NED HANLAN'S BOOK OF ROWING

The Rise and Fall of Canada's Little Giant

Edited by
JONATHAN SEILING

with
SIMEON SEILING

ISBN: 978-1-990827-18-1 pbk

978-1-990827-19-8 ebook

Gelassenheit Publications wishes to acknowledge Simeon J. Seiling as an editorial contributor, who significantly improved this book.

Cover image from *Canadian Illustrated News* [Vol. 20, no. 4 (July 26, 1879)] (Montreal: Burland-Desbarats Lithographic and Pub. Co.). https://www. canadiana.ca/view/oocihm.8_06230_506

Fas est et ab hoste doceri.
One must also be taught by enemies.

—Ovid

Non durius sed prudentius.
Smarter not harder.

—not Ovid

CONTENTS

PART II
RACE ANNOUNCEMENTS AND
REPORTS: 1878-1900 (SELECTIONS)

APPENDIX

CHRONOLOGY

1845
"Gaming Act" passes in the UK making gambling contracts
legally unenforceable with legal betting houses regulating
transactions (law is overturned in 2002)

1840s
John Hanlan (1821-1872), emigrates to Canada from Kilkenny,
Ireland, marries Mary Ann Gibbs (b.1823)

1849-52
Eldest sisters of Ned, born in Kingston, Ontario,
Mary Ann (1849) and Emily (1852)

1854
John Hanlan receives commission to repair a schooner at Toronto,
family sails there from Kingston and lives on the boat until a
storm tosses the boat across the bay to Toronto Island, where they
settle as the first leaseholders

1855
Edward ("Ned") born July 12, son of fisherman and hotelier John
Hanlan and Mary (Ann) Gibbs

1860
At age five Ned rows across from Toronto Island to the mainland to attend the public appearance of the Prince of Wales

1863
Railroad between Montreal and Windsor is completed

1871
Sliding seat is introduced, allegedly invented by two men independently: Walter Brown and J. C. Babcock

1872
Ned takes over the family hotel business after father's death

1873
At age 18 Hanlan wins amateur rowing **Championship of Toronto Bay**

1874
August 15, **Championship of Ontario** 'Lord Dufferin Medal', first professional race at Burlington Bay

August 15, 1874 Ned Hanlan wins first professional race on Burlington Bay, currently the location of Leander Boat Club

1875
Defends **Championship at Toronto Bay**

1876
Philadelphia regatta, Hanlan wins **Open Professional
Sculling Prize**
Group of local businessmen establishes "The Hanlan Club"

1877
October 15, **Championship of Canada** defeating Wallace
Ross in front of 25,000 Toronto spectators
Boston Silver Lake Regatta, July 4, Ned is defeated when
outrigger breaks mid-race
December 17, Ned marries Margaret Sutherland, bearing six
daughters and three sons (1879-1899)

1878
Ned defeats Fred Plaisted in Hamilton, Ontario
Championship of America title in Pittsburgh, vs. Ephraim
Morris, June 20
Championship of Maritime Provinces
Lachine, Quebec, vs. Charles Courtney

1879
May 5, John Hawdon, River Tyne, Newcastle
June 16, William Elliott, **English Championship** title and
The Sportsman's **Aquatic Challenge Cup**
August 18, Barrie Regatta, tie between Hanlan and James Riley,
but Hanlan refuses rematch
October 6-16, Lake Chautauqua in Mayville, NY, vs. Charles
Courtney

1880
November 6, International Regatta on Thames sponsored by an
American company
November 15, Hanlan beats Trickett on Thames also a **World
Championship Race** with 100,000 spectators

1881
February 14, beats Elias C. Laycock on Thames

1882
April 3, First **"Sportsman" Challenge Cup** beats R.W.Boyd
May 1, beats Edward Trickett

1883
May 31, Point of Pines Canada
July 18, Ogdensburg, N. Y.

1884
Travels to Australia, falls ill with typhoid fever and loses a title
race to Bill Beach, becomes **Champion Sculler of the World**
(Beach holds title 1884-1887)

1885
Hanlan challenges Beach for world title and loses
October 15, (doubles) Hanlan and G.W. Lee beats C. E. Courtney
and P.H. Conley near Albany, N.Y.
October 24, J. Teemer wins US title on Hudson River

1886
August 14, Lake Quinsigarnond regains **US title**

1887
Challenges Beach for a second time and loses again
May 30, challenges mentee Gaudaur and loses for championship
of America
July 23, defeats Gaudaur and regains **US title**

1888
August 13, loses US title to J. Teemer
May 5, challenges Kemp for world title and a £500 side bet,
Kemp wins by four lengths
September 28, challenges again for the title and another £500
side bet, loses by 12 lengths

1891

August 8, (doubles) Ed Hanlan and Wm. O'Connor beats J. G. Gaudaur and J. McKay, Hamilton Beach, Ontario

1892

October 15, J. G. Gaudaur and G. H. Hosmer beats Wm. O'Connor and Ed. Hanlan, Lake Couchiching
All sports betting is made illegal in Canada, with the exception of horse racing

1893

July 24, Hanlan challenges Gaudaur again for the US title and loses

1894

Hanlan's Point Amusement park is built

1897

Hanlan the first head coach of the University of Toronto Rowing Club
Hanlan Point Stadium is built as the home field for the Toronto Maple Leaf Baseball team

1898-99

Hanlan elected Alderman in Toronto

1900

Defeated in municipal election, leaves politics; seeks appointment as Toronto deputy Harbour Master, rejected, and coaches Union Boat Club of Boston and the crew of Columbia University, New York

1908

Ned Hanlan contracts pneumonia in January 1908 and dies at age of 52, over 10,000 people process by his coffin

1909
A fire destroys stadium and the hotel and Amusement park
burns down

1910
Hanlan's Point Stadium rebuilt in concrete

1914
September 5, Babe Ruth hits his first professional home run into
the waters of Lake Ontario from this stadium

1926
City of Toronto dedicates 6-metre statue of Ned Hanlan by
Emanuel Otto Hahn, on Toronto's waterfront

1937
Stadium demolished because of diminishing fans

1955
Inducted into Canada's Sports Hall of Fame

1969-1985
Betting restrictions begin to ease in Canada; more forms of sports
betting are made legal

2003
Statue of Hanlan is moved to Hanlan's Point

2016
Inducted into the Canadian Rowing Hall of Fame

2021
Betting law changes so that single-game sports betting is legal in
Canada:
Bill C-218, "The Safe and Regulated Sports Betting Act"

AN INTRO TO NED

JONATHAN SEILING, PHD

"QUIET, UNOSTENTATIOUS..."

… yet seen by some as a jerk, whose "clowning" was so intentionally loud and "showy", that it was surely meant to draw unruly crowds, including those who didn't dress the part or uphold *decorum*. Or was it? Was Ned's behaviour merely intended to goad and catch the ire of his opponents or perhaps to influence the sport's gambling odds, thus throwing the burgeoning world of betting into a tizzy? Whatever the causes, Ned would become the master at what we now know as the athlete-showman. He wasn't just a serious competitor, but a playful entertainer. At one point, his competitor even refused to race unless Hanlan promised not to embarrass him with the antics people expected from the short rower whose impact was supersized. There's little wonder why little Ned had a giant appeal while dividing fans and foes as to his character and motives. And no doubt, Ned changed the sport in no small way, giving Canada an athletic legend the world noticed.

In a sport showcasing the skill and speed of human-powered movement through water, some newcomers rooted a lower-class fisherman to dominate and deflate the sport's Ivy-league-style aires. Competition became open to all despite attempts by some to maintain the exclusivity of the sport. Lower-class competitors with no financial means to procure a decent boat were soon classified as "professionals" simply on the basis of their employment in any activity related to boating, including fishing and boat-building (See the Appendix under 'Definitions of an Amateur' from England, France and Germany).

The 1879 Henley definition sought to include under "professional" anyone who "ever taught, pursued, or assisted in athletic exercises of any kind as a means of gaining a livelihood" and even those who worked as an "artisan or labourer." Furthermore, anyone who had at any time entered a competition in which there was an entrance fee or prize money offered, even if the rower didn't win, was also deemed a professional. An amateur was exclusively an "officer of Her Majesty's army or navy or civil service, a member of the liberal professions, or of the Universities or Public schools, or of any established Boat- or Rowing-Club."[*]

The 1870s witnessed changes of all sorts: the evolution of construction materials, the mechanics of the boats (outriggers and sliding seats) and the opportunity for a new technique of rowing. The modern era introduced social elements into athletics with the participation of different races and social classes, where a Black fisherman could row the actual boat he used to catch fish, competing against wealthy athletes, who benefitted from the latest innovations in equipment. The rise of gambling transformed the sport, and likewise, the sport would also have an impact on how gambling was regulated. It was an era of mass change in society and this sport was part of that change.

One of Ned's boyhood mentors and friends on Toronto Island was Bob Berry, a fellow fisherman's son and local sculling champion who was a Black Canadian. Near the end of Ned's life, in 1907, he was paraded through the city alongside Tom Longboat, the Olympian, record-breaker and Boston marathon champion, born at Six-Nations who was Onondaga (Wolf clan).

And while it's unclear exactly whom Ned should have credited for teaching him to row, according to a report in the *Evening*

---

[*] Pieter Helbert Damsté and Frans Eduard Pels Rijcken, *Nederlandsch handboek voor roeisport* [Dutch manual for rowing sports] (Amsterdam: H.G. Bom, 1886), 11.

Telegram (January 6, 1908) it was Ned's sister Emma who taught him to row, albeit, before the invention of the sliding seat.

Local competitions gave rise to neighbourhood heroes, who were sent off for regional titles, and then national and international ones. In the years following advances in mass transportation and communication (1860s), the role of sport in shaping identities and moving finances into the realm of recreation and entertainment opened opportunities for newcomers of all kinds to find fame and fortune. The need for fairness and regulation soon involved lawyers, and legislators. In addition to prize money, rowers would often make side bets with their opponent, whereby the competitor signalled their personal stake in the race as a guard against throwing it for bettors.

Along with the heightened focus on athletics in society came the rise in this same era of so-called *yellow journalism* or *tabloids* in which sensationalism was the standard. Instead of reporting facts, writers sold more copy by drumming up interest through speculation, which also fuelled eagerness to put money on the line in legal or illegal betting forums. The spread of information deeply impacted the popularity of certain races and likewise influenced the placing of bets. Unfortunately, journalism in the late 1800s couldn't rely on cross-checking sources, so they weren't always accurate. For example, in the 1887 article about Jake Gaudaur's defeat of Hanlan, they stated Gaudaur's origin as St Louis, Missouri instead of Orillia, Ontario. Such glaring errors have been left in the texts, with endnotes to clarify. In such reports as we read from 1886, we can feel the frustration of the reporter, who wants to raise suspicions about malfeasance, yet complains that the details were intentionally kept secret.

YOU BET!

In 1883, the British Parliament revised its *Betting Act* (see Appendix) and given the controversy arising from Ned's small stature, the upsets his races caused in England, and the fact that Newcastle was both a centre of rowing in the United Kingdom and the location mentioned in the parliamentary debates on why the laws required amending, we might wonder, was Ned at the centre of this? The historical record may be a little light on the exact details, but we might guess that Ned's antics and the financial losses the opposing backers suffered were key contributing factors.* And if you're suspecting the author of this introduction aims to demonstrate yellow journalism in this comment, in which there's no solid evidence that Ned's antics led to an overhaul of the entire British Empire's approach to gambling, well, you bet!

Whether quiet or loud, unostentatious or a showman, Ned simply was a character, and a complicated one at that. Although he was considered shy in his younger years, an international career emboldened him to the point that when he later faced opposition, whether on the water or in City Hall as a politician, he had more verve and tenacity than egotism or entitlement. Most locals even called him "good-natured" and a national hero. The fact that his early days were also tarnished by a warrant for his arrest (bootlegging alcohol) seemed easily forgotten in time.

If stats are important, Ned's can hardly be rivalled by anyone in any sport. Most reports state that he rowed in 350 recorded races, and won 300 consecutively, but some set the total lower, at 200. One race he allegedly tied, or at least, it was declared a draw. Reportedly he only lost six official races, yet that number is not as easily determined when one consults the sources. As for the rest of the 350 or 200 that he won, the drama both on and off the racecourse could fill several volumes. (see below 'A Tie and A Few Losses')†

---

* For an historical overview of betting see D. Miers, *Regulating Commercial Gambling: Past, Present, and Future* (London: Oxford University Press, 2004).
† There is a surprising lack of clarity in the available sources, concerning the exact rowing records, including the championship titles. One helpful source for the world championships in rowing is from the Australian Rowing History website: https://www.rowinghistory-aus.info/world-pro-sculling/01-racing-record#gsc.tab=0. The website also contains several reports on key races, which are not found in this book.

"THOSE WERE THE DAYS"

Against the backdrop of economic, industrial, cultural and social evolutions in the British Commonwealth and American society, the introduction of the sliding seat changed the sculling technique. Some resisted while Ned earned the title "father of the sliding seat" for having taught the world how to use it to his advantage.* The sliding seat was reportedly invented in 1871, but Hanlan began racing professionally with a traditional seat.

During Hanlan's heyday, moving pictures were invented in 1878, and while photography was becoming more widespread, it wasn't until 1881 that the first camera film roll was available; the Kodak camera first appeared in 1888, the year after the gramophone allowed recorded sound to be re-projected. Given his photo-friendliness, Hanlan probably posed for more photos in a decade than most people after him did in their lifetimes, yet no videos of his famed rowing technique survive.

The only constant in those days was change. In communication, the invention of the postage stamp in 1836 was immediately overshadowed by the telegraph the following year, and in 1844 the introduction of Morse code, before the telephone changed the world in 1876.

In the 1820s, horse racing experienced the benefits of an improved stopwatch system and the introduction of binoculars. With electric lightbulbs (1878/79), modern society was poised to see the introduction of toilet paper (1880), the fountain pen (1884) and Coca-Cola (1886) in the same years as the first gas motorcycles, automobiles, steam turbines and electric streetcars also brought streets to life.

Other developments in communication and transportation allowed middle-class masses to glimpse more of the action than they could previously, and the sport of rowing adapted to inventions and social changes at an increasing rate during the height of the global Industrial Revolution.

---

* Frank Cosentino, *Ned Hanlan* (Don Mills: Fitzhenry & Whiteside, 1978), 12.

NATIONALLY PRIDEFUL

Amid the challenges of the newborn Dominion, Ned made a name for Canada on the world stage. When we consider Canada's appearance on the world stage, it is remarkable that Ned's championship at the Philadelphia regatta coincided with the year when A.G. Bell invented the telephone, exactly a century after the United States gained its independence as a nation.

While international consuls worked to entice the British public to emigrate to Canada, it was said that Hanlan's victories did more than all the agents heretofore combined and that he increased the value of the nation even more than the new railroad!* Both of those statements may seem exaggerated, but there's little doubt Wayne Gretzky did the same thing a century later to lure Russians from behind the Iron Curtain, who were envious of western rinks.

Ned's first professional race was on August 15, 1874, at Burlington Bay, which began Ned's meteoric rise with consistent victories over champions and winning successive titles. That happened to be the same year the first indoor hockey game was played, anywhere, ever. Oddly, the rise and fall of Ned's rowing career also paralleled the introduction of hockey in Canada, which speaks further to the age in which he lived. While Hanlan was making his professional career in athletics, the 1880s saw the rise of national hockey championship games and the awarding of Lord Stanley's Cup in 1888. By 1884, Ned lost his world title in rowing and 1887 made a failed attempt to regain it. By 1890 hockey players could also become professionals in the new national sport, which only fifteen years prior began to be held in an indoor setting.

---

* Cosentino, 29.

During the 1880s in the United
States an attempt was made to
adapt the sport of rowing to land,
resulting in a sport innovation that
seems to have had no traction. The
so-called "Road Sculler" was a
tricycle with a sliding seat,
propelled with a rowing motion,
patented by Daniel Kempster. In

'Road Sculler' debuted in 1888

1888, a competition event was held at Madison Square Gardens
in New York City, where some of the top scullers competed, and
while the list included Canadian Jacob Gaudaur, Hanlan was not
among them.

LITTLE GIANT

The 5'8" and 150-lb Irish-Canadian fisherman who transformed
the sport from Toronto Island was named Edward Hanlan at
birth. Little "Ned" rose to become a giant before he too was
toppled. A legend in his own time, his legacy is still debated today,
150 years later. Songs were composed (*Hanlan's Galop*, 1878,
Salomon Mazurette's *The Magic Boatman*, and *The Hanlan Waltzes*),
and before hockey cards appeared, cigarettes even offered trading
cards with his likeness!

LEGENDARILY SO

What sort of character was he according to reports in his day?
While it's true we all have different sides of our personality, which
come out in different ways at different times, given the sensation
surrounding Ned, some of his contemporaries and a few recent
writers have chosen to accentuate his ignoble sides. A century and
a half ago, it was left up to reporters to scribble down impressions
and conversations; people talked and word spread quickly and
Ned liked to give them lots to talk about! But today, the challenge
of sorting through these plentiful accounts is no small
undertaking.

It is evident in this collection of reports that some journalists were content to leave gaps and unanswered questions, that leave us guessing as to exactly what happened or what the journalist meant. Their attempt to sensationalize Ned may have done him and us a disservice. Others apparently had the privilege of speaking directly with Hanlan, but the journalistic standards of the day didn't require them to share with us exactly who provided this information and how reliable it was. Hanlan became a mix of legend and fact, a churning of news and rumour mills, creating waves and ripples in his wake.

Legends and facts ideally cohere, so that we may trust that a reputation rests on reality. The following collection leaves many gaps and it also provides overlapping accounts, such that some races will be described differently and some races are not found here. The task of the reader, hopefully an enjoyable pursuit, is to appreciate how each writer's attempt to convey information about past and upcoming races, came from a specific regional or national context. They loved the sport and the excitement surrounding it, as nations crossed the world to gather massive crowds and witness individuals and teams competing in a challenge involving speed and flair. It was one of the few international sports and the fact that cigarette packets featured rowing champions speaks volumes about its popularity in the late 1800s. Sports, like everything else including yellow journalism, became industrialized. We might wish we could view it on film, but we cannot. Thanks to these writers, we have colourful renderings of their perspectives on the legend that was Ned.

SILVER SCREEN SON-OF-A...

As a local hero, Hanlan was Canada's first international champion in an individual sport, and the press at home described him as *modest, charming, gracious, kindly, clean, humourous, honest and sporting.*[*]

---

[*] *The Globe*, quoted in: Wendy Lewis, *Fire on the Water: The Red-Hot Career of Superstar Rower Ned Hanlan* (Toronto: Lorimer & Co., 2007), 42-43.

In a poorly-researched bio-pic on Ned Hanlan called *The Boy in Blue* (1986), the mayor of Toronto hails the returning champ with those complimentary words after he returned as champion from the Philadelphia regatta in 1876. But up to that point, the film made it seem like Ned was a low-life criminal, a scoundrel and *persona non grata* in Canada. It is fairly clear those words spoken by the mayor were placed there by the scriptwriter as irony because until that point the film does its darndest to prove Ned Hanlan was an embarrassment to society — until he gave Toronto a reason to be proud, at which time he was embraced as their prodigal son! The film portrays Ned as a drinker, womanizer and bar-brawler, ill-suited for polite society until he rowed his way into public acceptance and people chose to ignore his past indiscretions. That's not how the actual story went, not according to the sources from that period, as can be read in the documents in this book. Surely Ned can be known in these pages as also honourable.

The legend of Ned centres around his comparatively small stature. However, in *The Boy in Blue* Hanlan was played by Nicolas Cage, the 6'0" all-American So-Cal playboy. The R-rated feature film reportedly cost $7.7 million, and the box office revenue drew less than a tenth ($0.7 million).

Here Ned is portrayed as an outlawed bootlegger, heavy drinker even at a young age, an occasional fine dresser and a philandering romancer who prefers to settle business and personal matters with his fists. Little Ned is discovered and reformed by a coach played by Christopher Plummer, who cannot rescue the recycled rags-to-riches sports narrative: the colonial trope of the feral-to-somewhat-tamer-underdog champion, who will supposedly inspire our young foals to grow up into hulking steeds who overcome the best of the best of the richest.

The film virtually ignores his international races outside of North America and his later career as a coach, businessman, politician and family man. It closes with an on-screen text, which, despite its brevity includes a few factual errors about the rest of his career, including, "on his retirement he ran for public office. He was elected by a landslide," as though his mere popularity was the main story. But it fails to mention that his tenacity and penchant to fight for good causes against industrial giants meant he would leave politics as quickly as he entered.

Whether it's true that he won by a landslide, his time in office was short-lived, not because he lost popularity but because he tried to stand up against industrial polluters. During his short time in office, he made various improvements for residents (bike paths, expanded streetcar service, public pools and a library), but when he condemned the harbour trust for its neglect of sewage and breakwater issues, he was soon forced out of office.[*] Ned also "advocated public ownership of the profitable ferry service despite it being managed by his brother-in-law."[†] The film offers nothing of this side of Ned, which also reflects the social context which shaped him.

While one might consider his defeat in 1884 to be his retirement from professional rowing, it actually wasn't. He challenged the world title holder twice again, the last being in 1887 and after years of coaching he rowed again in 1900, which is a tale the sources below will tell. All of this speaks of his character, which was complex and layered.

Finally, the irony of the film's title cannot be missed either: given that Hanlan's size was so noteworthy that his rise as a champion was through technique rather than sheer strength, the choice of *Boy* in the title, with the choice of the 6'0" Nicolas Cage as the actor, leads to the conclusion that the word 'boy' is meant as pejorative, rather than honouring Ned's lower-class background and character. He was a full-grown man. Since Cage was relatively tall, the film's title makes no sense otherwise. Whatever insights might be gained from the life of Ned Hanlan, it should be clear that the film will only confuse and distract us from the historical record and it speaks more to the distortions of Hollywood.

---

[*] http://www.biographi.ca/en/bio/hanlan_edward_13E.html
[†] "Ned Hanlan 1855 – 1908." June 24, 2020 Contributed from the Cabbagetown People Website – www.cabbagetownpeople.ca His resting place can be found in the Necropolis @ Section C, Lot 40.
  http://pstreetnews.com/education-news-toronto/ned-hanlan-1855-1908/

BUT IN FACT!

Few authors have analyzed the available sources to provide book-length accounts of Hanlan's life, and they are not widely available. Aside from some excellent summary articles written over the past fifty years,* the best full-length overview is the book by Wendy Lewis, *Fire on the Water,*† which provides an overview of Hanlan's life and significance in a terse volume written for young readers in a balanced and compelling way. In 1978, Frank Cosentino previously wrote a short, helpful biography, also aimed at a young readership.‡ Otherwise, beyond the various biographical articles, original accounts of his races aren't readily available in print.

THE BOY BEFORE THE MAN

There is scarcely a telling of Hanlan's life without mentioning his legendary feat in September 1860: "He first made the newspapers at age five when he rowed a skiff to Market Wharf across a bay

---

* Frank Cosentino, "Ned Hanlan – Canada's premier oarsman; a case study in 19th century professionalism," *Canadian Journal of Hist. of Sport and Physical Education*, 5 (1974), no.2: 5–17; Andrea Brown, "Edward Hanlan, the world sculling champion, visits Australia," *Canadian Journal of Hist. of Sport and Physical Education* (Windsor, Ont.), 11 (1980), no.2: 1–44; J. M. Schwartz, "Ned Hanlan: portrait of a sports hero," *Archivist* (Ottawa), 15 (1988), no.4: 7–9. *Standard dict. of Canadian biog.* (Roberts and Tunnell); Richard Macfarlane 'Row for Glory: Canada's Ned Hanlan stayed one stroke ahead of controversy to become the world's fastest man on water.' Posted June 3, 2015 https://www.canadashistory.-ca/explore/arts-culture-society/row-for-glory; Bruce Kidd, "HANLAN, Edward (Ned)," in *Dictionary of Canadian Biography*, vol. 13, University of Toronto/Université Laval, 2003–, accessed August 14, 2024, https://www.bi-ographi.ca/en/bio/hanlan_edward_13E.html.
  Two excellent articles by the Toronto Reference Library Blog in 2015 and 2018: "Toronto's First Sporting Hero: Ned Hanlan," July 15, 2015, author "Nicole" https://torontopubliclibrary.typepad.-com/trl/2015/07/torontos-first-sporting-hero-ned-hanlan.html and "Remembering Edward 'Ned' Hanlan. July 12: Snapshots in History" July 13, 2018, author "John P." https://torontopubliclibrary.typepad.com/local-history-genealogy/2018/07/remembering-edward-ned-hanlan-july-12-snapshots-in-history.html
† Wendy Lewis, *Fire on the Water: The Red-Hot Career of Superstar Rower Ned Hanlan* (2007).
‡ Frank Cosentino, *Ned Hanlan* (Don Mills: Fitzhenry & Whiteside, 1978).

crowded with vessels awaiting the arrival of the Prince of Wales."[*] Tales about being born in a boat or learning to row before he could walk are fantasy, but they make the point that his genius was nurtured from the beginning of his life on Toronto Island.

He was the third of four children, having two older sisters and a younger brother. He also rowed himself to school and brought fish to market, where he had a chance to race other fishermen vying for the early-bird customers. In addition to being a fisherman, his father was a boat builder and he passed these skills on to Ned who later built one of his own racing shells.[†] His father became the police constable of the Island and also built a small hotel there, which Ned took over when his father died (1872), amid Ned's rising career as a professional rower. It was at this time that the Hanlan Club was formed by supporters in Toronto to support his professional career.

His boyhood social context reveals that growing up in the lower-income community of fishermen, he had plenty of experience as an underdog. Bob Berry, an African Canadian neighbour who was a few years older than 13-year-old neighbour Ned, surprised everyone in 1868 by winning the race at the Championship of Toronto Bay. But Berry was disqualified for allegedly rounding the buoy improperly. Two years later Berry won the race and held the title.[‡] Hanlan would later encounter another rower who was Black, a star from the southern U.S. who was nicknamed "Frenchy" Johnson (I've found no source which actually states his real first name).[§] His protégé, Jacob Gaudaur, who later won the world title and followed in Ned's shoes, was of Métis and Scottish ancestry. Rowing became anything but an elite, exclusive sport in Ned's era.

---

[*] Bruce Kidd, "HANLAN, Edward," in *Dictionary of Canadian Biography*, vol. 13, University of Toronto/Université Laval, 2003–, accessed May 11, 2024, http://www.biographi.ca/en/bio/hanlan_edward_13E.html.
[†] Lewis, 28.
[‡] Lewis, 19-25.
[§] Eric Cordon, "Frenchy Johnson: From Slavery to Sporting Champion," https://thewestendmuseum.org/history/era/west-boston/frenchy-johnson-from-slavery-to-sporting-champion/

NORTH AMERICAN TITLES

At Toronto and Hamilton, Hanlan stepped into the title races as a young man of 18, and continued to fish while he ran his family's small hotel business. By the time he turned 19, he won a series of races, which settled his position as the Champion of Ontario. The *Hanlan Club* supported his training and organized his equipment and finances, to prepare him for bigger races. At age 21, he was ready for the Centennial Regatta in Philadelphia, celebrating the 1776 Declaration of Independence. It was quite a moment for a young, little-known Canadian to step into the American limelight.

Yet due to an arrest warrant for bootlegging, Ned had been unable to train for the race in the previous weeks while hiding from the police. As such, Ned arrived at the regatta as a virtual unknown and set a new record at the regatta. Reportedly, his welcome back in Toronto was akin to that of a victorious military general, including parties, a parade, and a silver medal and gold watch from the mayor, as the ink on his arrest warrant somehow faded from the page.[*]

December 17, 1877, Ned married Margaret Gordon Sutherland, who was born in Pictou, Nova Scotia a coastal town near New Glasgow. He now shifted his racing activities to New York State and faced the American, Fred Plaisted at the upcoming Silver Lake Regatta in Boston. Ned lost because his outrigger snapped during the race while ahead of Plaisted, and he had to watch his rival cross the finish line first. Why did it snap? Let the rumours fly!

Two weeks later a rematch was set for the rowers, but Plaisted refused to show and Ned won by default. Plaisted refused again to be challenged, until the July 4th Regatta in Boston. Likely harbouring revolutionary ideals as a son of liberty, inspired by the lingering tannins of anti-colonial tea parties from the century past, Plaisted finally faced Canada's little giant on the banks of Beantown, in a race that resulted in riotous protests. After what sounds like a chaotic and dangerous spat of melee, each calling

---

[*] Lewis, 38-42.

foul on the other, Ned was banned from racing in Boston. Upon appeal, the ban was lifted, but the label of "exceedingly unbecoming" behaviour was firmly attached to Ned.[*]

The next two major races led to the "Championship of Canada" (October 15, 1877), and after defeating Plaisted again in Hamilton (May 1878), he won the "Championship of America" title in Pittsburgh (June 20, 1878).

The next chapter of further drama came with the challenge by the American Charles Courtney (Mayville NY, October 16, 1879), at a high-profile race where Hanlan's boat broke apart during the pre-race training. Then, the night before the actual race, despite having guards stationed at the boathouse, Courtney's boat was sawed in half. It was reported the guards went to the casino. Despite being offered a replacement boat, Courtney refused to race and then vanished.[†]

Soon afterward, Ned was accused of offering a bribe to Courtney to throw the race, and in return, Ned stated that the opposite was the case, that Ned had been offered (and refused) a bribe. They didn't race until the next year on the Potomac in Washington, D.C. with a crowd of about 100,000 fans, including the U.S. President, watching nervously to see if the race might lead north and threaten another Gettysburg battle, with not-so-distant memories of General Lee's 1863 boat crossing.

With Hanlan far in the lead, having completed the first half and now turning back to retrace the course toward the finish line, Courtney and the third rower, Riley, both turned back before reaching the halfway marker, which the crowd also saw. It then appeared that Courtney was in the lead but Hanlan still managed to defeat them both, despite their blatant attempt to cheat. Perhaps only to accentuate the absurdity, Riley then claimed he could have defeated Hanlan, so another race was set, in which Hanlan beat Riley by half a kilometre.[‡] For anyone who still

———————————

[*]   Lewis, 46-47.
[†]   Cosentino, 38-41.
[‡]   Lewis, 77-81.

boycotts the metric system, half a kilometre is roughly equal to five NFL fields.[*]

NED VS. NED FOR THE WORLD TITLE

In Australia, another Ned at that time claimed the title of world rowing champion. Edward Trickett won the world title from the British, Joseph Sadler in 1876. At 6'4" the Aussie Ned was a portrait of contrasts beside the Canuck as they raced on the Thames that flowed through their colonial capital on November 15, 1880. If Hanlan expected a gentlemanly matchup, despite being notorious for his playful antics, he was seemingly unprepared for the boasting, bragging, mocking, chaffing and bluffing of Trickett's friends while training. Ned complained they nearly tossed him over the edge at one point — whether that was meant psychologically, or simply a toss into the water, it's not clear from the quote.[†]

Despite all of their foreplay, the Aussies allegedly offered Hanlan a bribe to throw the match, which would have made Hanlan a very wealthy man. When he defeated Trickett, whose last name seemed apt, Hanlan displayed antics and diversions including zig-zags. It made the race sound more like a Harlem Globetrotters production than a world title race. His clowning earned him little respect among the establishment but he became a sensation among the crowds in England.

Elias Laycock, another Australian, who won London's International Regatta, at which Hanlan was asked not to compete, challenged Ned and requested that he refrain from the need to embarrass him. As requested, on February 14, 1881, Ned beat him by four boat lengths and said he considered Laycock "a decent plucky man."[‡]

In 1882, Ned accepted two challenges to take place in

---

[*] Or 39 lengths of the original Stars and Stripes "Old Glory" (42').

[†] Lewis, 85.

[‡] Lewis, 93.

England on the Tyne, from Trickett and Robert Boyd, who held the English title in 1877. Making a mid-race display of rigorously cleaning out his sinuses, Hanlan, ever the crowd-pleaser, easily won against Boyd, but instead of clowning against Trickett, he rowed to the finish a minute and a half ahead. At that point, speeding back to where Trickett was, Hanlan made an about-face and sped a second time to the finish line, to beat him twice in the same race.* In the face of all title challenges over the next two years, the little giant stood tall.

Ned held the title for four years until he fell ill with typhoid fever and promptly lost against another Aussie, William Beach, on August 16. Ned immediately challenged for a rematch. Again, he lost. As Frank Cosentino wrote: "Hanlan's feats have been shrouded in cultural amnesia which surrounds many Canadian heroes. As the young nation was attempting to forge a union with links of steel, Hanlan's accomplishments made the National Dream manifest on the individual level."†

POST-PRO

Ned turned to a career of coaching the sport he had transformed (Ottawa, Toronto, Boston and New York), and then entered local politics in 1898. As an Alderman of Ward 4 in Toronto, he was appointed to the Harbour Trust. He and his wife Maggie also raised a bunch of kids during these years: Edith, May, Grace, Audrey, Margaret, Aileen, Douglas, and Edward Gordon (another son died in 1888 as a toddler).

Up until 1900, he occasionally attempted title challenges, including to his protégé, the Canadian, Jacob Gaudaur.

When Ned caught pneumonia at age 52, his death soon followed and on December 17, 1908, Canada lost its athletic giant, who, according to *The Globe*, "practically taught the world to row."‡ As a more recent commemorator claims, Hanlan was the

---

*   Lewis, 99.
†   Cosentino, 62. Photograph: https://www.loc.gov/resource/pga.03498/?st= image
‡   Lewis, 106.

Brady-Handy photograph collection,
Library of Congress, Prints and
Photographs Division.

"most discussed and best known Canadian throughout the world" when "rowing was by far the most popular sport in the young Dominion" in the second half of the 1800s. He claims "Canadian excellence in the sport fired the young nation's collective imagination and enabled Canadians to measure their country within the family of nations."* If that is the case, nascent nations the world over and Canadians looking for where our nationhood is best defined might want to grab a pair of oars — or at least plop onto a rowing machine for a few minutes — to get a taste of this simple, meditative yet all too often exclusive and even rarified or elitist sport. In its heyday, rowing seemed capable of overcoming barriers of race and class. What does Ned's story amid Canada's ongoing search for identity and purpose, say about the role of sports as a social glue, one that perhaps replaced religion and also broke down divisions of class and race, at this phase in its development?

In Ned's day, the popular summer sports of English Canadian society had been rowing, cricket and horse racing. In general, all these sports were uppity and it's perhaps a sign of his age, that after conquering rowing, society could break away from the feigned decorum of these sports in favour of a puck-on-stick battle in winter, when the weather left the burly less employment and the task of writing epic poetry about Ned Hanlan had already been accomplished (see Appendix, *Hanlan's Record*).

In an era when an older sister taught the world champion to row, when Black Canadian and Black American rowers made their mark on the sport, whilst Yalevard still contended with

---

* Cosentino, 3.

Oxbridge for dominance, the Irish-Canadian fisherman lad, a shy Islander just off the coast of *Toronto the Good* was as tall as any 5'8 ³/⁴" man might ever hope to stand.

The Toronto Harbour still dons a boating club, but the baseball stadium is a very distant memory and the Island airport watches planes fly where Babe Ruth's famous first-ever homerun was sent into the lake. If Ned were to learn that Hanlan's Point on Toronto Island later became famous as Ontario's only nude beach, we might imagine his combination of delight, bewilderment and temptation for antics. Perhaps the beach Hanlan's Point could someday be renamed "Cagey Point" with free public viewings of *The Boy in Blue*, because otherwise, the R-rated film about this legendary rower will be unavailable unless one is willing to pay $250 online for a Blueray copy (such is the availability at the time of this writing).

A TIE AND A FEW LOSSES

Ned had a stunning record of wins, and while the number of races he won ranges from 200 to almost 350, there seems to be no complete record available, which could verify such stats. Any notion of a streak of 200 races is quite difficult to fathom, given the losses that periodically appear in the chronology. While the list below is likely incomplete, it is an attempt to list the races Hanlan is reported to have lost. The task of listing 300+ wins will fall to a future writer.

Each race Ned failed to win has its tale to tell. We don't know all the details of all of them, although some are provided in the reports below. It has been stated that he only lost six races, but the count is probably double that, especially if one includes the doubles competitions in which he also competed.

It is noteworthy that Jacob (Jake or Jack) Gaudaur, the Canadian who won the world title in 1896, defeated Hanlan in 1887 for the U.S. title, and they held various races in which Hanlan did not always win. Against the Australian William (Bill) Beach, Hanlan also lost in a fair race, even while beleaguered by his recovery from typhoid fever. Later he also lost to the

American, John Teemer already in 1885 and again in 1887. In 1888, Hanlan lost to Kemp in Australia, and in 1892 lost in doubles to Gaudaur and Hosmer. In 1896 his boat also collapsed in a race at Halifax.

If we count the two races in 1877 at Boston, then a tie and a loss in 1879, after he lost the world title and the other titles he held, and the challenges in which he failed to regain titles, there were closer to a dozen lost races. In some cases, there were fouls or upsets during the race, where the fastest racer was not necessarily the winner, but it seems the ones surrounded by the most controversy were against Americans. He struggled with a handful of Americans (for any European readers, this means the "non-Canadian" kind of American, just like Ned's dad was a non-Brit from the British Isles, meaning the "Atlantic Archipelago"), and he had some friction with at least one Aussie, as recounted in the documents below. The popularity of W. E. Harding's 1880 book, *Edward Hanlan: America's Champion Oarsman* might be partly to blame for confusing the world as to the Irish-Canadian's national affiliation.

The race at the Barrie Regatta, August 18, 1879, against James Riley has been described as a botched attempt by Riley to "throw" the race, because Riley reportedly bet on Hanlan, against himself. Also, Hanlan had recently returned from Europe and was not fit. Halfway through the race Hanlan stopped and said he was unable to finish and clearly would have lost. But Riley then refused to cross the finish line and despite being ordered to re-row, Hanlan also refused, preferring to forfeit the prize money.* Such bizarre tales don't seem so strange when we dig to uncover other sports scandals, which continue to the present day.

In summary, excluding the Barrie regatta against Riley, Ned's losses were as follows:

1876: June 13, Silver Lake Regatta in Boston, vs. Fred Plaisted, Hanlan's oar outrigger broke, allowing Plaisted to catch up and win.

---

* Cosentino, 38.

1877, July 4 Regatta in Boston, Hanlan collided with Plaisted's boat, leading to his disqualification.

1880: June 17, Lost at "Hop Bitters" Regatta Rhode Island (due to illness)

1884: August 16, defeated in Australia by William Beach, on the Paramatta course where he was obstructed by a steamer; lost the World title, and immediately challenged for a rematch and lost.

1885: October 24 lost to Teemer at Pleasure Island, NY (his boat was swamped); May 28, lost challenge to Beach

1887: Gaudaur beat Ned by 2 seconds to win the American Championship title at Pullman, IL; later the same year, defeated Gaudaur at Pullman; August 13, lost US title to Teemer at Toronto; November 26, lost to Beach on Nepean River, Australia

1888: May 5, Lost to Kemp on Paramatta course, Australia (Hanlan was fouled); September 28, subsequent loss to Kemp, with another foul; November 27, lost to Beach

1890: Lost to Gaudaur at Duluth

1892: doubles (Hanlan and O'Connor) lost to Gaudaur and Hosmer at Orillia

1893: July 24, lost to Gaudaur at Orillia

1896: boat collapsed in Halifax race

BABE RUTH'S FIRST CAREER HOMERUN AGAINST LEAFS AT HANLAN STADIUM

Toronto Daily Star, *September 7, 1914*

A few years after Ned Hanlan died, the baseball stadium on the island at Hanlan's Point hosted the Toronto professional baseball team called *The Leafs*. Babe Ruth's first career home run was launched into Lake Ontario from Hanlan's Point Stadium in 1914.

❧ I ❧

I: ACCORDING TO HIS FELLOWS

CHARACTER IN FRAGMENTS

THE QUIET "DUDE"

*Those who know Hanlan best describe him as a quiet, unostentatious man, and in proof of this the following anecdote goes some distance. Some of the members of a rowing club in the States went out for exercise, and, just as they were getting into a boat, they noticed a "dude" standing on the bank, faultlessly attired. "Boys," said the stroke, "let's take the dude down." The stranger was accordingly put into the boat and told to keep time as near as he could with the stroke, and that the exercise would do him a world of good. Away the boys went, the "dude" sawing along, but managed to keep good time for a novice. Faster and faster they went, but still the "dude" hadn't even doffed his vest, while with the others, though in boating costume, it was a case of "bellows to mend." The stroke kept piling it on till something like 46 was reached at the finish, but they couldn't knock "dude" out.

---

* *Edward Hanlan, champion oarsman, with history and portrait* (Albert S. Manders & Co., Melbourne, 1884), 20.

NB: The two editions of this book, which appeared first in New York in 1880 and later in Melbourne in 1884, differ in content and pagination. The 1884 Melbourne edition is quoted below, when it contains material not found in the 1880 New York edition by Wm. E. Harding, the Sporting Editor of the *Police Gazette*, of New York, Richard K. Fox, Publisher, No. 183 William street, New York (New York, 1880).

Then the boat stopped, and as the crew looked round the "dude" asked in a quiet tone, "Well, gentlemen, when do you reckon to do your final spurt?" For a moment they were speechless, and then the stroke asked, "Who in the name of Jehosophat are you?"

"Well, gentlemen, my name is Edward Hanlan. I'm from Toronto, and at present on my way to Australia. Good day."

IDENTITY

*When rowing on the Nepean, in training for the match with Laycock, he was paddling up and stopped opposite a certain part, from which he was going to row to another, a half-mile distance; as a boat previously to him reached the first post, Laycock and his brother were rowing up at a good pace. As Hanlan was fixing his watch to time himself, he perceived two men sitting on the bank, when the following dialogue took place:

> Broad Irish on bank: "And be sure who is that as is just gone up?"
> Hanlan: "That's Laycock of course."
> B. I.: "And what time will Hanlan be out?"
> Hanlan: "He is out, and where I am."
> B. I.: "You, Hanlan! to blazes with you! what, are you gammoning us; that be blowed, you are not Hanlan."
> Hanlan: "Well gentlemen if you don't believe me I can't help it."

And with that Hanlan went off at a rattling pace like a shot from a gun, doing the half-mile in 2.45 min.

---

* *Edward Hanlan, champion oarsman, with history and portrait* (Albert S. Manders & Co., Melbourne, 1884), 38.

THE BETTER MAN

*Hanlan avers that Laycock was the best man he had ever met. "If," said the champion, "I can row as well when I reach his age I shall be more than satisfied."

Hanlan states that he has never, except on one occasion, had to row harder in a match than he and on the Nepean. This was when he met Trickett on the Thames, and the explanation is not that Trickett is a better man than Laycock, but that he (Hanlan) was never in worse form for a race than on that particular occasion. He explains that when Trickett "went to pieces" in the race he was very near doing the same thing, but lasted a little longer than the Australian, and won.

MUST BE PRONOUNCED THE...

†Ned Hanlan must be pronounced the Shakespeare, the Napoleon, the Michael Angelo, the Bismarck of the Oarsmen. However, he ought to wash his face before starting a race.

RESTING IN PEACE

‡The most famous Canadian of his day, he was idolised in Toronto. In both 1898 and 1899, he was elected an alderman. On January 4, 1908, Ned Hanlan died of pneumonia. In his lifetime, he took part in approximately 350 recorded races, losing only six and tying one!

---

*   *Edward Hanlan, champion oarsman, with history and portrait* (Albert S. Manders & Co., Melbourne, 1884), 21.
†   *Buffalo Courier,* quoted in Cosentino, 35.
‡   *Section C, Lot 40, Toronto Necropolis.* https://www.mountpleasantgroup.com/en-CA/General-Information/Our-Monthly-Story/story-archives/toronto-necropolis/ned-hanlan.aspx

KING NED OF THE CANADAS

*The Canadians have reason to be proud of their man, and if there was an elective monarchy established in the Dominion we have no doubt that a majority of votes would be given to "Ned I., King of the Canadas."

WARMEST SPORTING PROCLIVITIES

†In 1878, the *Napanee Beaver*: "There are two single individuals that have done most to bring Canada into prominence in the quarters where that prominence will most avail. They are Lord Dufferin and Edward Hanlan. … Edward Hanlan by his victories with the oars, has as a Canadian oarsman appealed strongly to the hearts of a nation having the warmest sporting proclivities."

NAPOLEON OF ROWING

‡Hanlan may be truly called the Napoleon of rowing, not only because of his consummate skill, but also because of his having revolutionized the methods of training, the style of rowing, and of rigging sculls. At the Centennial at Philadelphia, while yet a lad, he brought over with him new ideas and rigging, shorter oars, and wider blades. When one considers that he was the first to go out against the world, and a boy at that, one can readily understand the amazement of the world, congregated at the famous exhibition, at finding him easily a minute faster over a 3-mile course than the best that England or America could produce. He had strength of purpose enough, too, to throw to the winds of all the previously held ideas on training. Up to the time of his advent into the rowing world – and he had a dose of it too – the prevalent methods of training prescribed raw beef steak, dry

---

* Quoted from a New York newspaper, Cosentino, 52.
† Cited in https://myemail.constantcontact.com/All-the-News-from-the-Hanlan-Boat-Club---January-2021.html?soid=1131350406857&aid=bTrVLjTzOhc
‡ *Montreal Herald,* Feb 3, 1900.

toast, and half a cup of tea. He soon did away with that sort of fare and dieted himself on good, wholesome, fare and lots of it. The result has been that he has kept strong and vigourous and was enabled, while actively engaged to travel about night and day to fill engagements. A thing to be remembered in connection with his career is that in his time rowing was most popular, at the same time represented by scores of the very best athletes that the world could afford. Hanlan has rowed over twenty-five match races in a single summer, and he found it difficult to get from place to place fast enough.

"MUNT-REEL" LOCATED IN ICE

*Perhaps the full value of the work done by Hanlan in the line of advertising Canada has never been fully realized. It was not until his third trip to England that the papers changed their headings from "The Yankee Sculler" to "The Canadian Rower." Australia furnished some very amusing incidents. On his arrival there on his first visit, everything in sight from the Parliament buildings to ash carts, were profusely decorated with the stars and stripes. The reception he received there, which was a gorgeous affair in itself, was a mere *bagatelle* as compared with the enthusiastic reception accorded him there. The only idea that even educated Australians had of Canada was a hazy notion of the residence of some such as Sir John A MacDonald and the faint rumour that a village called Munt-Reel was fixed in ice somewhere near the North Pole.

---

* *Montreal Herald*, Feb 3, 1900.

TOTAL TECHNIQUE

GRACE AND POWER

*The style in which Hanlan moves his oars when recovering from
the stroke, although having no effect on his rowing, must attract
notice. The broad blades skim so close to the surface of the water
that they are scarcely seen, and it is one of the neat actions which
in combination give such a finish to his rowing. Feathering is one
of the strong points with amateurs. Some oarsmen give
considerable attention to this minor point while calmly ignoring
all rules for getting extra pace from the boat. Some of the Sydney
scullers put plenty of power into their strokes, but recover in a
slovenly way that mars their style, while perhaps in no degree
interfering with effect, Hanlan, however, combines grace with
power, and unites the tasteful feathering of the amateur
enamoured of fancy rowing with the long powerful strokes of the
champion. …

On the water, Hanlan and his boat are as much in harmony as
an animate and inanimate object can be. His sliding is as
methodical and regular and as free from apparent effort as the
motion of the driving shaft of a locomotive engine when running

---

*   [no author] *Edward Hanlan, Champion oarsman, with history and portrait* (Albert S.
Manders & Co., Melbourne, 1884), 21.

at the regular rate of speed. His oars strike the water and leave it at the same rate of speed; and here, again, his action reminds one of a machine that may be slowed or quickened to certain rates of speed, but which never otherwise varies its action. It is only in "spurting"—an effort seldom required in his contests—that Hanlan loses his mechanical action. Then he seems to double himself as a greyhound does for a spring, and the way the oars dash through the water, and the light shell answers to those powerful sweeps is a treat to witness. That spurt was only seen twice during the late race, and then more by way of an exhibition than because there was any real necessity for it.

*"**...**worth travelling a hundred miles to see and was just as good as the others was weak."

SHARP, CLEAN 'CATCH'

†Hanlan claims that any oarsman, to become an expert, must row as follows:

> A full, long reach out over the toes, with both arms straight; a sharp, clean 'catch' of the water; a powerful, steady, horizontal stroke, with an application of the whole force at the moment of immersion; a clean feather and a low, quick recover, shooting out at the moment of the finish. Good form is especially desirable, and this can only be gained by steady practice. Some professionals claim that the long slide to the seat is the best, but among the crack oars the short slide is being adopted. It is of the greatest importance in a long race that the lower part of the chest should be as free as possible, otherwise the wind will not

---

* Wm. E. Harding, *Edward Hanlan: America's Champion Oarsman* (New York: Richard K. Fox, 1880), 25.
† Wm. E. Harding, *Edward Hanlan* (1880), 7.

last. It has been shown that the best way to hold out in a long race is to keep the back straight, head erect, shoulders thrown back and stomach out. Oarsmen should bend from the hip, and not double themselves up; if one does he is certain to lose the action of the lower part of the lungs. The head should be up and eyes in the boat; nothing is so bad as to have any member of a crew turning or looking around. The knees should be spread well apart, thereby giving the loins an easy, and more powerful action. In commencing a stroke, the arms should be straight and at full length.

There are many faults to be avoided in handling the oar, one of the most important being the dropping of the hands too low at the end of the recover. Another fault is that of dipping too deep, very common in beginners, and caused partly from raising the hands in the middle of the stroke instead of pulling the oar straight through the water. The oar should be put on its face, the inner part slightly turned toward the water. In this way, only the blade of the oar will be immersed, and at the finish will come out cleanly without lugging or danger of crabs. Of the forward reach and dip, the best authorities on rowing say: When the forward reach is taken the blade of the oar should travel backwards in the air after the dip, horizontally, at a distance of a few inches from the water, of course the distance depending whether the water is rough or smooth. As regards the dip, the blade should descend to the proper depth before any force is applied, otherwise the stroke will cut. To effect this the hands must be raised sharply, and the stroke must commence at once.

DIFFERENT TO ANYTHING HITHERTO SEEN

*Hanlan has abolished the cross-handed style. He has shortened his sculls inboard considerably, and what he has taken off at the handles he has put into the blades. His style of pulling, too, is different to anything hitherto seen, and it is wonderful with what

---

* Wm. E. Harding, *Edward Hanlan* (1880), 25.

clock-like regularity he swings backward and forward, impelling his boat through the water with a force that seems truly marvelous when compared with the apparently small amount of power. In Trickett's rowing the case is very different. There the motor can be clearly traced, and a novice can tell where the power is being put, and, great sculler as Trickett undoubtedly is, he evidently lacks the knowledge of how to equalize his enormous strength like Hanlan. There is a lack of that harmony of the members which the casual beholder cannot fail to perceive when Hanlan reaches forward or swings backward with the finish of the stroke.

UNIVERSAL WONDER AND SURPRISE

*All the champion oars men and wielders of the "spruce" have been compelled to succumb to his wonderful prowess at the oar.

Wallace Ross, Charles E. Courtney, John Hawdon, William Elliott, James Riley, Edwards and Trickett — United States, Canada, England and Australia, have all been compelled to acknowledge Hanlan's supremacy over them with the oar.

The question now arises, are all these wonderful victories the result of skill, dexterity and muscular development, or have models, systems and methods played an important part. Hanlan's victories over oarsmen who were in many cases his superior physically have created universal wonder and surprise.

The secret is, Hanlan is one of the most finished scullers that ever sat in a shell. By constant practice and invention, he has become master of a style which it will take years for oarsmen to copy. He rows without the least apparent fatigue or exertion, and although an opponent may do twice as much work, and strain himself to a pitch of muscular tension, his shell will fail to travel as fast as Hanlan's.

Hanlan's style, practice, and his knowledge of the oar from long and tried experience, has been the means of his success.

English oarsmen, prior to Hanlan's invasion of England, boasted that their style was the best. Joseph H. Sadler, in 1870,

---

*   Wm. E. Harding, *Edward Hanlan* (1880), 3.

came here from England and easily defeated every oarsman who dared meet him. Trickett then visited England, and by slight improvements in his shell, combined with muscle and extra strength, defeated Sadler. Since that time a great advancement has been made in boat building in America. Sliding seats, invented by Walter Brown, one of America's champion oarsmen, have been improved, patent out-riggers and swivel rowlocks have been invented and also added to American racing shells, so that English oarsmen are behind the age, as they failed to adopt the American inventions. These advantages, in a measure, have gained for Hanlan the proud title of champion of the world, and created a revolution in the building of racing shells and the style of rowing among boating men in England.

BESTRIDES HALF A TON

*Hanlan's speed in a shell is amazing. He is not a very big man, nor all over a powerful one, though he is exceptionally well developed, not only where an oarsman always wants it in the loins but where one who rows as he does absolutely must have it in the extensor muscles of the legs. For he does not kick his stretcher, or shove his feet against it with anything like a jerk; but he sets them against it and pushes with the heaviest and mightiest force he can possibly apply, much as a man pushes with his legs and feet upon the floor when he bestrides half a ton and lifts it if he can. This supreme push, far more forceful than any sudden kick could be, throws every ounce of pressure against that fulcrum that he can possibly impose. Hence he gets more power into his work than any less effective pusher could get, and it rushes him forward accordingly. This is largely why thirty-six of his strokes send him faster than forty-one of Trickett's, and put him two good lengths to the front before either is off the Crab Tree, and while both are comparatively fresh. It is hard work and accounts for Hanlan's many stops to rest, but it does the business. It looks about hopeless for a rower on the old method to try to cope with him. It really

---

* Wm. E. Harding, *Edward Hanlan* (1880), 27.

need not be so, for at least to the more intelligent among the rowing men it must seem astonishing that a man like Trickett, a professional, who has for years been champion of the world, has not sense and judgment enough to let such a rusher go on about his business, and instead of trying like a freshman to catch him by crazy spurts at the start, so distribute his strength and wind as to carry him his fastest, whatever that may be, over the whole four miles and three furlongs, not over a paltry half mile. For, as usual in Hanlan's races, the time over the whole course is slow, though marvelously fast for a little way as long as it is necessary. If on that dead flat water, and with the current as it was, Trickett and his friends had not thought before the fight he could have done the distance in less than twenty-five minutes they would probably never have let him leave Australia. And yet his little rival thrashes him hopelessly, and makes a laughing stock of him in twenty-six minutes and twelve seconds. There is a lesson for Oxford and Cambridge in all this. There is a lesson for Harvard and Yale in it, and for every oarsman or sculler, amateur or professional, whoever means to row a race. Let us see who will first learn it.

THOROUGHLY SCIENTIFIC

*Hanlan's style, good though it undoubtedly was, appeared to even greater advantage when seen alongside of the miserable form of our professionals. Hanlan was a well-made man, of middle height, and a thoroughly scientific sculler. He was the best exponent of sliding-seat sculling among professionals, only a long way so; but we, who can recall Kelley and Chambers in their best days, must hold to the opinion that the two latter were, ceteris paribus, as good professors of fixed-seat sculling as ever was Hanlan of the art on a slide. Had sliding seats been in vogue in 1860, and the next half-dozen years, we believe that Kelley and Chambers would have proved themselves capable of doing much the same that Hanlan did in his own generation.

---

* W.B. Woodgate, Boating, 2nd Ed. (London: Longmans, Green & Co., 1889), 228.

We have seen Kelley scull on a sliding seat. He was fat and short of wind, and never attempted to make a study of the leg work of sliding; but, being simply an amateur at it, his style was a model for all our young school to copy. Like all old fixed-seat oarsmen who have attained merit in the old school, he stuck to his traditional body swing, and added the slide to it, as it were instinctively. There could hardly be a greater contrast of action than to see scullers like Boyd or Blackman kicking backwards and forwards, with piston action and helpless bodies doubled up at the finish, and to observe, paddling within sight of these, old stagers like Biffen and Kelley in a double-sculling boat fitted with slides. It was easy to see that until the new generation of British professionals could be taught first principles of rowing on a fixed seat, there was small chance of their ever acquiring the proper use of the slide as exemplified by Hanlan.

BACKSTORY AND BUILD

* The "Little Giant," as the friends of Edward Hanlan love to call
him, is one of the most remarkably formed men in the world.
Considerably below the full stature accorded to man, he looks
even shorter than the figures given by his tape line. His shoulders
are not so broad as they ought to be in comparison with his other
proportions, and in his "store clothes" there is little to mark him as
a prince among athletes and oarsmen. But when stripped for a
race, and the thin, tight-fitting costume of battle reveals the
secrets of his almost abnormally developed hips, his wonderful
back, and his magnificent arms, then it is that the mystery is
solved, and one cannot help feeling that the aquatic hopes of the
Dominion of Canada are founded upon a rock. A handsome face,
but hard, and an eye which is capable of the most vindictive
lights, are eloquent and truthful tokens that he is a most
determined and ugly antagonist. He goes into a race to win, and
he means to win it whether by fair means or foul.

Edward Hanlan is an Irish Canadian, and was born in the
City of Toronto, his present place of residence, on the 12th day
of July, 1855. While Ned was yet a child his parents removed to
the long, low strip of land now known as Hanlan's Island, which

---

* W. E. Harding, *Hanlan vs Courtney: A Guide to the Race of 1879* (Buffalo: Baker,
Jones & Co., 1879), 18-19.

forms the Toronto Harbor. This gave him the needed facilities for boating, and he was soon more at home over his oars than in his father's house. Naturally enough he fell into the way of amateur oarsmen, and at the age of sixteen he was one of a strong crew of fishermen.

Although doing work here which excited the envy of his companions, he was not known outside of a very limited circle. When he was eighteen years of age he tried his fortunes in a shell, rowing against Williams and McKen, two local favorites, for the championship of Toronto Bay, and whipping them both soundly. With such a start his thoughts were naturally turned into the channel of professional oarsmanship, and when in 1874 he battled with Thomas Louden for the championship of Burlington Bay, he showed that money was no drawback upon his prowess.

* ... born at Toronto, July 12, 1855, and while quite young was taken by his parents to the Island opposite the city, where his father opened a hotel, and where the family have ever since resided. He is 5$^{ft.}$ 8 $^{3/4 in.}$ in height.

His first appearance in a race was made when he was sixteen years of age, when he formed one of a crew composed of fishermen. In the following year he figured as a successful competitor in a couple of skiff races, and in 1873 first rowed a race in a shell, the contest being for the amateur championship of the Bay. He was again victorious, defeating Sam Williams and McKen. Next year he met Thomas Louden in a race for the championship of Burlington Bay, this being his initial professional engagement. The result added another to his list of victories. Louden challenged him to row another race, over a mile course, for $100 dollars a side, in the summer of 1875, and they met on Toronto Bay, Hanlan again showing himself to be the better man, as he won by nearly two lengths. During the same season, he won a medal offered by the Governor General in a two-mile pull at

---

* W.H.C. Kerr, Hanlan's Record: an epic poem (Toronto: Belfords, Clarke & Co., 1879), 9-14.

Toronto, defeating Louden and James Douglas. In the spring of 1876 he vanquished Douglas and Wm. McKen, and on August 12th following became possessed of the belt emblematic of the championship of Ontario, offered by the Toronto Rowing Club, his only opponent being McKen. At this regatta Hanlan likewise won a fisherman's race, three pairs of sculls, his partners being McKen and Elliott, and the craft engaged being boats actually in use that summer. All of these races were of minor importance, however, and the reputation they brought was but local.

It remained for Hanlan to give the rowing world a startling surprise at the Centennial regatta on the Schuylkill River, when his name became known on both sides of the Atlantic, through the ease with which he won the first prize in the professional regatta, defeating Harry Coulter, Pat Luther, Plaisted, and easily disposing of Alex Brayley in the final heat, which was rowed in $21:09^{1/2}$—the best three-mile time on record until Courtney cut down the figures last year. In March, 1877, the Secretary of the Ontario Rowing Club forwarded to the *Clipper* Office one hundred dollars in gold as a deposit for a proposed match between Hanlan and Billy Scharff (then champion), to row three miles, for $1,000 a side, on Toronto Bay; but as Scharff had just made a match with Eph. Morris, the challenge from the Canadian was not accepted.

Hanlan next appeared at the regatta held at Silver Lake, near Boston, Mass., June 18th, when he was defeated by Fred Plaisted, Frenchy Johnson, and others, owing to a mishap in the shape of an injured outrigger.

On June 25th another regatta was held on the same water, when Hanlan won first prize, beating Johnson and Driscoll, Plaisted not starting. The Kanuck next took part in the scullers' race at the Boston Fourth-of-July regatta, and was ruled out for fouling Plaisted, whom he ran into at the turning stake. His conduct on this occasion gave great offence to the regatta officials, who subsequently passed a resolution recommending that in future Hanlan be debarred from participation in all races under municipal management. This action was, however, upon appeal from Hanlan himself, and through representations of gentlemen who had taken him in hand after his return to Canada, reconsidered, and the bar against him removed.

After the victory of Ross over Brayley in the fastest time on record for four miles, the Toronto sculler published a challenge to Ross, whose backers were not prepared to talk business on this basis. However, Wallace's defeat of Plaisted, coupled with the indifferent performances of Hanlan at Boston and vicinity, inspired them with greater confidence, and about the middle of August, Ross came out with a challenge to row any man in the Dominion. Hanlan preferred a five-mile race for $1,000 a side, offering to give or take $300 for expenses, to row at St. John, N.B., or Toronto, or to row at Springfield, Massachusetts, each paying his own expenses. This suited Hanlan, and articles were signed to contend for $1,000 a side. They pulled the race on Monday afternoon, Oct. 15th, on Toronto Bay, five miles, one turn, for $2,000 and the championship of the British Provinces, the result being a very hollow victory for Hanlan, who was the non-favourite, but easily rowed away from his man.

Wednesday afternoon, one May 15th, the sculling match between Hanlan and Fred A. Plaisted, of New York City, for $1,000 a side, was decided over a straight-away two-mile course on Toronto Bay, the former again achieving a hollow victory. No official time was taken, and the reports estimated it all the way from 13:14 to 15:12. On June 20th the race between Hanlan and Evan Morris, of Pittsburg, for the championship of America, five miles, was decided on the Alleghany River, and proved an easy victory for the former.

Hanlan's next event was his second match with Wallace Ross, which, after repeated postponements, came off on the Kennebeccasis course on July 31st last. At the first mile stake Ross fell overboard, and left the race a walkover for the Toronto champion. The race was for $1,000 a side, five miles with a turn. Two weeks after, on August 12th, Hanlan was first in the professional scull race, four miles, $1,000, of the Barrie Regatta Club, rowed on Kempenfeldt Bay, Wallace Ross taking second money, and George H. Hosmer, of Boston, third. The contestants who failed to get a place were Pat Luther, McKen, Elliot, Plaisted, Morris, and Coulter.

His next contest was that at Lachine, in which he defeated Charles E. Courtney, the Union Springs sculler. The event, which took place on the 3rd of October last, created a great deal of excitement because of the fame attaching to both contestants. The race was a keen one and resulted in favour of Hanlan, time 36 min. 22 sec.; distance five miles. But Hanlan's as yet greatest victory—although it was a very easy one—was that rowed with John Hawdon, of Delaval, on the Tyne, on the 5th of May last. The Toronto boy on that occasion came in as he pleased, his time being 32 min. 5 sec. He was five lengths ahead at the close, but he might have led by half a mile if he had been so inclined.

* "a waist like an oak's trunk" — "The muscles of his legs stood out like bunches of cable chains and glided like serpents beneath the bronzed skin that covered them. Such a perfect specimen of manhood ... is seldom seen."

† Edward Hanlan was born in Toronto, on July 12th, 1855, but while he was still an infant his parents removed to the Island, which has continued as the home of the family ever since. Prior to his coming out as a professional sculler Hanlan divided his time between fishing and looking after the hotel which his father had opened on the Island not long after he first moved thither. From his childhood the Canadian champion, though very fond of manly sports, has always been industrious, temperate and very correct in his habits and conduct. He stands five feet eight and three-quarter inches, and has rowed most of his races at from 148 to 154 lbs., though perhaps 152 or 153 lbs. would be considered his best weight for a hard race.

---

* From *The Globe*, 1880, quoted in Lewis, 82.
† Wm. E. Harding, *Edward Hanlan: America's Champion Oarsman* (New York: Richard K. Fox, 1880), 3.

From his childhood Hanlan was very much on the water; and when quite young became ambitious to win fame as an oarsman. His first attempts at rowing with outriggers were made in a very novel craft of his own design and construction. It was a two-inch plank sharpened at both ends, and furnished with a slightly elevated seat and outriggers. Though uniformly successful in his earlier engagements, Hanlan was singularly slow in obtaining the fame and reputation that his abilities as an oarsman fairly merited.

...

Hanlan resides at Toronto, Canada. He has been made a freeholder, and the Canadians presented him with a free lease of the island opposite Toronto, and they also presented him with his home, which cost over $20,000. Hanlan has a large circle of social friends. He is gentlemanly in his manners, and wherever he goes boating men honor him. While in London, England, he gained a host of friends. It will be a long time before another oarsman crosses the Atlantic and wins the honors and laurels for his country as Hanlan did.

Hanlan is one of the greatest oarsmen that ever appeared. He is in his golden prime, and what may be done with a pair of sculls and a racing boat he can do. He is a man of very symmetrical build, muscular and strong without being clumsy, his wind is good, his constitution excellent. He abounds in resolution, and he is conformable to the wishes of his trainer. At the same time he weighs more, when in condition, than many think. When he beat Courtney one of the sage reporters of this city described him as a boy, the fact being that he was bigger and heavier than Tom Sayers, champion of England, had ever been, in fighting condition, in his life.

Hanlan's victory, or rather his series of victories, teaches a lesson, of course. He is not nearly so powerful-looking a man as Trickett, or as half a dozen oars men whom he has defeated. A man, however, is like a machine. He is just as strong as his weakest part. Great muscles are of little use if there are not lungs equally good to back them, and powerful lungs are next to nothing in a race if heart and other organs are not fully as able to bear their part of the strain. Hanlan is like the deacons celebrated "one-horse shay." All his parts are equally balanced. Every muscle seems to be just as strong as its fellow, and probably when Hanlan gives way he will go altogether, as the "one-horse shay" did.

Hanlan bears the same relation to the art of rowing that Rowell does to that of walking. As in Rowell's case, his victories have always left the extent of his powers a matter of conjecture. Neither of the athletes has ever been pushed to his utmost, and each has been satisfied to merely win his event and leave the definite measure of his abilities undecided.

* Hanlan ... began his rowing career at the early age of 17, when he won two skiff races. In 1873, he competed in a wager boat race for an amateur championship and defeated two pullers named Williams and M'Kay. He commenced his professional career in 1874 and 1875, when he rowed and beat Thomas Louden and in the latter year won a gold medal given by the Governor General of Canada, beating Louden and Douglass. In 1877 he beat J. Douglass and W. M'Ken and in August of the same year won the Championship of Ontario, and was also in the crew that won a fisherman's race (three pairs of sculls) at the same meeting. These were but local races, however, his great victories commencing from the date of the Centennial Regatta at Schuylkill, where he won the first prize, heating the renowned H. Coulter, Luther, Plaisted, and Green, of London, in the trial heats, and easily defeated Brayley in the final. At the regatta on Silver Lake, Boston, Mass., in 1877, through his outrigger getting injured, he was defeated by Fred Plaisted and others. In a regatta at the same place a few weeks afterwards, he won the first prize, for which Plaisted entered, but did not start. On October 15, 1877, Hanlan rowed Ross a five-mile race for the championship of the British Provinces and a stake of 2,000 dollars, winning easily. His reputation now became fixed, and he found friends among some prominent gentlemen in Toronto, into whose hands he placed

---

* 'The Sculling Championship of the World,' *The Argus* (Melbourne, Vic.: 1848 - 1957), 23 May, 1884, p. 6.

himself, with the object of their making all arrangements for his events in the year 1878, their intention being to make matches with the leading scullers of England and Australia. Among those to whom the challenges were directed were Edward Trickett, Evan Morris, W. Scharff, of Pittsburgh; and John Higgins and R. W. Boyd, of England; the result of these challenges being that Hanlan rowed and easily defeated Plaisted on Toronto Bay in a two-mile race for 1,000 dollars aside.

He next beat Evan Morris for the championship of America and 1,000 dollars aside at Hulton, Pa., on June 20. On July 1, at Brookville, he won the first prize of 500 dollars in a regatta open to all but Courtney. In this contest he defeated Plaisted, Kennedy, Riley, Ten Eyck, M'Ken, Luther, and Elliott. On July 4, he defeated Plaisted, Kennedy, and M'Ken for a 200-dollar first prize at Cape St. Vincent, N.Y. On July 31, he rowed Wallace Ross at St. John, N.S., for 1,000 dollars aside. In this race the water was extremely rough, and Ross got capsized. Hanlan next appeared at a regatta on Kempenfeldt Bay, Ontario, when he won the first prize of 500 dollars, Ross being second, Hosmer third, Plaisted fifth, M'Ken sixth, Morris seventh, Elliott eight, and H. Coulter last.

Following this great match, he rowed C. Courtney on October 3, for the championship and $5,000 dollars aside, defeating him by a length and a quarter. On May 6, 1879, he beat John Hawdon on the Tyne for 2,000 dollars. In the following June he beat Elliott for the Sportsman's Challenge Cup 2,000 dollars, and the English championship, on the Tyne. Returning to America, he rowed a dead heat with Riley for a 500-dollar prize. Hanlan, not being in condition, refused to row over again, and allowed Riley to take the prize. In May next he beat Courteney in a match for 6,000 dollars at Washington, and on the 26th of the same month defeated J. Riley at the same place for a stake of 2,000 dollars. At Providence, Rhode Island, he could not gain first honors for the Hop Bitters Prize, which was won by Ross, with Riley second. On the 15th November he beat E. Trickett, in a match for £200 aside the Sportsman's Challenge Trophy, and the championship of

England, and on February 14, 1881, beat Elias Laycock, of
Sydney, in a match for £1,000.

His next victory was on the 3rd April on the Tyne, when he
beat Boyd for a stake of £1,000. He met Trickett once more on
the 1st May following for £500 and won easily, and within the
next twelve months in America he successively beat Kennedy,
Hosmer, and Ross. At the time of his race with Laycock he had
not rowed since August last, when he competed at Massachusetts
with several oarsmen, but his boat was swamped by a passing
steamer, and Teemer won.

*Great muscle strength, we have already said, is not a main
requirement. As proof of this statement we refer to the fact that so
many great rowers of lesser physical strength have shown
themselves to be the masters of others who had much greater
physical strength. A striking example was Robert Coombes, a man
of very small stature and only 56¼kg, who won the
Championship of England in 1846, and was the first rower of his
time. And if we take Hanlan himself, what difference of physical
strength is there between him and Trickett, Laycock, Ross and
other giants, all of whom lost against him.

---

* Pieter Helbert Damsté and Frans Eduard Pels Rijcken, *Nederlandsch handboek
voor roeisport* [Dutch manual for rowing sports] (Amsterdam: H.G. Bom, 1886),
110-111.

RACE SUMMARIES: 1872-96

In the following section, four writers from different regions provide a summary of the career highlights of Hanlan's races, from his rise to his fall.

*1872: His first appearance in a race was made when he was sixteen years of age, forming one of a crew composed of fishermen.

1873: In the following year, he figured as a successful competitor in a couple of skiff races, and in 1873 first rowed a race in a shell, the contest being for the amateur championship of the bay. He was again victorious, defeating Sam Williams and McKen.

1874: Next year he met Thomas Louden in a race for the championship of Burlington Bay, this being his initial professional engagement. The result added another to his list of victories.

1875: Louden challenged him to row another race over a mile course for $100 a side, in the summer of 1875, and they met on Toronto Bay, Hanlan again showing himself to be the better man,

---

* Wm. E. Harding, *Edward Hanlan: America's Champion Oarsman* (New York: Richard K. Fox, 1880), 8.

winning by nearly two lengths. During the same season, he won a medal offered by the Governor-General, in a two-mile pull at Toronto, defeating Louden and James Douglas.

1876: In the spring of 1876, he vanquished Douglas and Wm. McKen, and on August 12th following became possessed of the belt emblematic of the championship of Ontario, offered by the Toronto Rowing Club, his only opponent being McKen. At this regatta Hanlan likewise won a fisherman's race, three pair of sculls, his partners being McKen and A. Elliott, and the craft engaged being boats actually in use that summer. All of these races were of minor importance, however, and the reputation they brought was but local.

Hanlan at this time became ambitious, and he decided to enter the International Centennial Regatta held at Philadelphia in 1876. Among the United States oarsmen entered to row in the single scull race, which was for the Championship of the World, was Patrick Luther of Pittsburg, F. A. Plaisted of New York, and Harry Coulter of Manchester, Penn., the ex-champion of America. Besides, Halifax also sent Alexander Brayley, their champion, who was confident of success.

Hanlan quietly went to Philadelphia and without the least pomp or display entered into training for the race. The great event was decided, and Hanlan won easily, rowing the three miles in 21m. 9$^{1/2}$s., beating the fastest time on record. After this great victory, Hanlan's name became famous all over the world, and he was looked upon as a wonder.

In the trial heats of the regatta Hanlan defeated Harry Coulter, Pat Luther, Plaisted, and easily disposed of Alex Brayley in the final heat. When Hanlan left his native city for the Centennial Regatta both he and his friends were heartily laughed at for their temerity in starting an unknown callow boy against a lot of seasoned professionals. When he came back, however, a great change had come over public opinion concerning him, and a torchlight procession and a very handsome testimonial awaited him.

1877: In March 1877, the Secretary of the Ontario Rowing Club forwarded one hundred dollars in gold as a deposit for a proposed match between Hanlan and Billy Scharff (then champion) to row three miles, for $1,000 a side on Toronto Bay; but as Scharff had just made a match. with Eph Morris, the challenge from the Canadian was not accepted. Hanlan next appeared at the regatta held on Silver Lake, near Boston, Massachusetts, June 13, when he was defeated by Fred Plaisted, Frenchy Johnson, and others, meeting with a mishap in the shape of an injured outrigger. On June 25th another regatta was held on the same water, when Hanlan won first prize, beating Johnson and Driscoll, Plaisted not starting.

Hanlan then visited Boston, Mass., and on July 4th, 1877, he participated in the single scull race at the Citizens Association Rowing Regatta held on the Charles River, Boston, and was ruled out for fouling Plaisted, whom he ran into at the turning-stake. His conduct upon this occasion gave great offence to the regatta officials, who subsequently passed a resolution recommending that in future Hanlan be debarred from participation in all races under municipal management. This action was, however, upon appeal from Hanlan himself, and through representations of gentlemen who had taken him in hand after his return to Canada, reconsidered, and the bar against him removed. After the victory of Wallace Ross over Alexander Brayley in the fastest time on record for four miles, the Toronto sculler published a challenge to Ross, whose backers were not prepared to talk business on this basis. However, Ross's defeat of F. A. Plaisted of New York, coupled with the indifferent performances of Hanlan at Boston and vicinity, inspired them with greater confidence, and about the middle of August Ross came out with a challenge to row any man in the Dominion, Hanlan preferred, a five-mile race for $1,000 a side, offering to give or take $300 for expenses, to row at St John, N.B., or Toronto; or to row at Springfield, Massachusetts, each paying his own expenses. This suited Hanlan, and articles were signed to contend for $1,000 a side.

This race was the real turning point in Hanlan's career. True, his performance at the Centennial had for the time placed him very high in public estimation, but his want of success in the Eastern regattas had done much to shake public confidence in his abilities. Though supported by good men for this contest with Ross, he did not receive anything like that care and attention which he has since come to regard as a matter of course. The boat he had was a very indifferent sort of craft, manufactured by George Warin, of Toronto, and whatever attention it required he had to bestow upon himself. In those days, instead of having his food carefully selected for him by a thoroughly competent trainer, he used to walk out to the butcher stalls and select his own steaks. He had good friends who stuck by him, though on the very day of the race, October 15th, 1877, a majority of those who had placed their money upon him weakened and hedged out as much as they could, gladly giving $100 to $75 in favor of Ross. In spite of all these discouragements, however, Hanlan's matchless pluck and coolness never forsook him. He took his work regularly as clock-work, ate heartily, and actually took such a satisfactory siesta after an early dinner on the day of the race that he had to be waked out of a sound sleep to go out upon the water and row down the man who was selling in the pools at $100 to $75, and this at a time when Hanlan well knew that many who had been his staunchest supporters were hedging out what they had invested on him just as fast as they could find takers at the odds just quoted. When the word "go" was given Hanlan was determined no mistakes should occur so far as he was concerned. He shot right to the front, and drawing away from Ross with the utmost ease, won without any trouble, making a melancholy exhibition of Ross, who was evidently in no kind of shape for the contest.

1878: At Toronto Bay, on May 15, 1878, Hanlan met F. A. Plaisted of New York City, in a two-mile race, straightaway, for $2,000. Hanlan won easily, and made such a laughing stock of Plaisted's abilities as an oarsman, that the judges did not take the time.

Hanlan's next race was for the championship of America, for which he had challenged the then-famous sculler Evan Morris, of Pittsburg. This race took place on the Hulton course, Allegheny

River, near Pittsburg. This was perhaps the hardest race Hanlan
ever had in a match. It was five miles with a turn, that is, they
rowed two and a half miles down the river and then back to the
starting point against the current, which was a very stiff one.
Morris came far short of being as good a man as Hanlan that day,
but the course was very much in his favor. Of course, any novice
might row down to the turning buoys with the current easily
enough, but it took a pilot to creep along close to the bank and
take advantage of all the little inshore eddies on the way back to
the starting flags. Hanlan had the race won, however, before the
turn was made, for, contrary to the expectations of the Hanlan
party, Morris made his grand effort when pulling down with the
current, and he was dead beaten before he turned his buoy. He
struggled on gamely to the finish and made such a terrible effort
to retrieve his fortunes that it is very doubtful if he has ever been
the same man since.

Hanlan did not rest long after his championship victory. On July
1st, 1878, he won the first honors at Brockville, beating Plaisted,
Riley, Ten Eyck, Pat Luther, John A. Kennedy, McKen, and
Elliott, in a race of four miles with a turn.

On the Fourth of July following he beat nearly the same lot of
scullers in a regatta at Cape Vincent. In both these regattas
Hanlan had it all his own way from start to finish.

Without returning to Toronto after winning first money in the two
regattas just mentioned, Hanlan crossed over from Cape Vincent
to Kingston, and thence made his way eastward to St. John, N. B.,
where he was matched against his old rival, Wallace Ross. The
race was to take place on the Kennebecasis, some seven miles
above the city, and Hanlan was soon quartered close to the water
side in the cozy and comfortable old Claremont House,
Torryburn, the very house in which the great Renforth breathed
his last.

Here Hanlan had just the climate, food and accommodation that
appeared to suit him best. He had plenty of time to put himself in
perfect trim, as (notwithstanding the two regattas in which he had
rowed) he had been enjoying an almost entire let up since the race
for the championship. It was while he was at the Claremont

House that the Canadian champion could do almost any amount of work, eat incredible quantities of the very best food, enjoy absolutely perfect digestion and sleep sound, dreamless sleeps. Here, when pointed for the race, he was as hard as nails, though he weighed somewhere about 154 or 155 lbs., while at Pittsburg he only scaled 148 lbs. when in rowing trim. Though no pains were taken to time Hanlan during his stay on the Kennebeccasis, his friends accidentally learned enough of what he could do to make them think from that time forward that when right and fit he could row down any man that ever lived.

After numerous postponements on account of rough water, the race finally came off on July 31st, 1878. The distance was five miles with a turn, for $2,000. At the start, Wallace Ross went away with the lead, but held it for barely a quarter of a mile. They both went a tremendous clip, however, but when they had gone a little over a mile, and when Hanlan was leading by fully two lengths, Ross rolled out of his boat, and it only remained for Hanlan to paddle over the course and claim the money.

Hanlan's next appearance was at the Barrie regatta, August 12, 1878, where he won first money, Wallace Ross coming second, and Hosmer third. The other contestants were Evan Morris, Harry Coulter, Pat Luther, Fred Plaisted, Wm. McKen, Alex. Elliott, and Edward Ross.

DECADENCE OF HIGH-CLASS ENGLISH

*While our sportsmen lament the decadence of high-class English rowing the name of one amongst our rivals has become famous as the embodiment of extreme skill and although Hanlan was not invariably successful the balance of his victories over reverses has been so decisive as to justify our giving him the palm.

Edward Hanlan is just thirty years old having been born in Toronto on the 12th of July 1855. His parents were of Irish origin and during the earlier part of his rowing career the name was written *Hanlon* but on his first reaching England in February 1879

---

* *Baily's magazine of sports and pastimes*, Volume 44, 1885, 492-494.

it appeared with two 'a's and has since been invariably written
Hanlan. His father keeping a hostelrie on an island near the city
the future champion was accustomed to the water and developed
quite early a taste for rowing, an art which he constantly practised
while following the business of a fisherman. He made his début
when only sixteen winning with two brother fishermen a race for
three pairs of sculls. In 1873 he competed for the Amateur
Championship of Toronto Bay and after some further triumphs
started on a professional career which he inaugurated by winning
a double scull race in Burlington Bay.

At the Centennial International Regatta held at Philadelphia
in 1876 where amateur and professional oarsmen of various
nationalities assembled and the English contingent were treated
with conspicuous unfairness, the Toronto sculler won the principal
open event and after some minor reverses ascended in the scale by
beating in October 1877 Wallace Ross for the Championship of
Canada. Ross was and is probably the second best sculler in the
world as on many occasions he has shown powers superior to
anyone barring Hanlan, whose next important engagement was
with Courtney. This elegant but unreliable oarsman had like
Hanlan started as an amateur and having taken to professional
sculling the men were matched to row five miles for the
Championship of the United States. The race was to all
appearances a very close one, Hanlan winning by a bare length
but he was generally thought to have a bit in hand anyhow. No
match could be arranged in America so he visited England and
took on John Hawdon of Delaval, a northerner then reckoned a
very promising candidate in a contest for £200 a side on the Tyne
early in May 1879. A challenge had in the meantime been issued
on behalf of an unknown to row the then champion of England
William Elliott for £200 a side and a Challenge Cup given by the
Sportsman newspaper and before the decision of the Hawdon
match which resulted in an easy win for the Canadian. It was
pretty generally known that he would figure as the so called
unknown so that unusual attention was bestowed upon the
practice of the new arrival. It was not to be expected that
authorities would agree as to the merits of Hanlan's style and

special mechanism of which a very long slide and swivel rowlocks were the prominent features. Elliott it must be admitted did his best to master the changes and succeeded fairly well though in the race itself he was never formidable, Hanlan leading from the first and winning as he liked by over ten lengths in the fastest recorded time for the Tyne course 21 minutes 21 seconds.

After this triumph Hanlan soon returned to America leaving England in July and after grand doings in New York was received at Toronto with boundless enthusiasm, a public subscription being raised to present him with his homestead at a cost of four thousand pounds. After some minor affairs in America he was challenged by Edward Trickett of Sydney New South Wales and a match arranged on the Thames course for £200 a side and the *Challenge Cup.*

The Australian on his first visit to England in 1876 had achieved his object the attainment of the Championship then held by Joseph Sadler an elegant sculler but confessedly past his prime. Trickett against whom odds of about 3 to 1 were laid won very easily but was careful not to try conclusions with any one else although the backers of John Higgins offered odds to tempt him and he returned to Australia declining all offers. Hanlan now being Champion of England was challenged by Trickett and a match arranged which took place on the 11th November 1880 when Hanlan won all the way. This race was remarkable not merely from the skill displayed by the winner but for the confidence of the Australian party who, relying upon Hanlan being "got at" either physically or pecuniarily, offered large amounts on their man until on the eve of the match even money on Trickett went begging at Putney.

Next morning when any arrangement proved impracticable the aspect was vastly changed from 2 to 3 to 1 being laid on the Toronto man. Trickett's companion Laycock having won a Hop Bitters prize against all comers now challenged Hanlan, who though desirous of returning home was greatly pressed to give the second Australian a chance and after an infinity of what passes amongst professionals as diplomacy and finesse a match was made between Hanlan and Laycock for a "monkey" a side and the possession of the *Sportsman* Challenge Cup.

This took place on the 14th of February 1881, when Hanlan again won with consummate ease and returned home Early in the following year however, he was back in England, R W Boyd of Newcastle flattering himself that he had become in skill and sliding more Hanlanesque than Hanlan and making a match for a thousand on the Tyne in April 1882. Hanlan after a few yards led easily and won as he pleased but the Australian ex-champion Trickett found friends to support him in another struggle with Hanlan, who in May again beat him from start to finish. Since these achievements the subject of our sketch has not visited England where indeed, sad to say, he is not at present likely to find a worthy foeman but has taken part in sundry minor affairs as well as in matches with Beach, now champion of Australia who beat him twice. Hanlan's latest performance was in a regatta at Geneva, New York where he beat McKay Hamm and Hosmer, Transatlantic scullers of repute in a three-mile race.

Hanlan is a well-knit man of medium height perfectly proportioned and in his manners and behaviour stands out as markedly from our notions of a professional rower as did Henry Kelley from his contemporaries in a bygone era.

DUTCH ROWING MANUAL

*It seems to us that at the beginning of a manual on the theory of rowing, a brief explanation of the history of this beautiful physical exercise should not be missed.

However, we would be groping around in the dark if we were to look for sources from which to trace the origins and gradual development; only a barren, empty plain would present itself to the researcher.

But there are oases in that desert. Those oases are the rowing competitions. These have been carefully recorded in ancient

---

* Pieter Helbert Damsté and Frans Eduard Pels Rijcken, *Nederlandsch handboek voor roeisport* [Dutch manual for rowing sports] (Amsterdam: H.G. Bom, 1886).

times, either as interesting facts in popular chronicles or as songs by admiring poets. And so the historian, going from match to match, can note the progress made in the dark gaps, and draw conclusions from them with certainty.

The competitions are our sources. How and when are these set?

As soon as many people start practicing an art, it will not be long before they will try to see which of them has achieved it furthest. At first such an experiment may perhaps be taken by chance, but soon the matter will find favor with several people, who are attracted by the desire for honor and fame, and soon fixed days or festivals are fixed for these experiments. ....

Most matches between professionals take place as a result of a challenge from one of the two parties for a certain sum.

Until 1876 an Englishman always had the title *Championsculler of the World*, but in that year J. H. Sadler was defeated by the famous Australian E. Trickett, who by this victory *the Championship of the World* and took £400 back to his homeland.

This sculler was born in 1851 in Greenwich on the Paramatta. In 1875 he became *Champion of Australia* and in 1876 an enterprising and wealthy Sidney hotelkeeper brought him to England and into the fray against the English champion Sadler.

After the success achieved there, he won many new laurels, until he entered the *Sidney-Regatta*, in which he took part while ill, and was beaten by another well-known Australian, Laycock.

After his recovery, however, he clearly proved his superiority. Yet he would not retain the proud title for much longer.

But the danger no longer threatened him from England: it would be a [North] American who had to transfer the honour of "having the best rower in the world" from Australia to Canada.

This man was Edward Hanlan.

Born in Toronto in July 1855, he won his first victory in a match for the *Amateur Championship in the Toronto Bay*. He then turned professional. In 1877, Wallace Ross, the celebrated sculler of the United States, challenged all the rowers of Canada to row a race with him of 5 miles for 1,000 dollars. Hanlan accepted this and won easily.

This victory, which made him *Champion of Canada*, suddenly drew everyone's attention, so that in Toronto the *Hanlan-Club* took on his further leadership. Now Hanlan had nothing left to worry about. The Club closed all agreements for him, took care of his needs in the nicest way, paid his travel and accommodation expenses, gave him the best trainers, in short, regarded him as their most precious treasure.

In 1878 he beat the New York sculler Plaisted for 2000 Dollars, then Evan Morris for 1000 Dollars and the *Championship* of all America, then again Wallace Ross and finally Courtney.

In 1879 he went to England to row against the English champion W. Elliott.

In order that the *Hanlan-Club* could make as much money as possible from the business, they made an agreement in advance, according to which Hanlan would first row with Hawdon, an English sculler of the second rank, and the victor in this match would compete with Elliott. The ruse was completely successful: the English, who did not know Hanlan, bet heavily on their champion, and the lords of the *Hanlan-Club*, who had all come over, took all bets.

When Hawdon was easily defeated, the English did not suspect anything, as Hanlan had not had to make any effort, so they continued to bet on Elliott. But there he also defeated Elliott on June 16, without the slightest difficulty, giving him the *Sportsman Challenge Cup* and captured £400, in addition to the *Championship of England*, and English gold flowed into the pockets of the [North] Americans.

On his return to Toronto, he was publicly festooned by the mayor, and the citizens presented him with a house costing 20,000 Dollars.

In 1880 he captured the *Championship of the World*. This match took place on the Thames and is recorded in the annals of rowing as one of the most important facts. Interested people flocked from three continents to watch the matchup, and it must have been an embarrassing sight for the English on their old Thames to see an American and Australian fighting for the title that one of their own had previously held.

But after 1876 the English were never able to lift themselves up again as far as professional rowing was concerned.

In 1881 he defeated Laycock, who had in the meantime defeated Trickett and therefore thought he could also take on Hanlan, with the greatest of ease and again on the Thames.

In 1882 he crossed again to England and defeated the English Champion Boyd and Trickett again.

In 1883 he won in America against Kennedy, W. Ross and many others.

In May 1884 he defeated Laycock again.

But this same year would prove fatal for him and would gaze upon the setting of the sun of his fortune.

The message in the "*Wassersport*" about his defeat began with the words:

> *Es fiel ein Stern herunter*
> *Aus seiner funkelnden Höh'*
> A star fell down
> From its sparkling height

And so it was. Hanlan had finally met his master.

It was William Beach who beat him at the Paramatta near Sydney for £500 and the *Championship of the World* up on the 16th of August 1884. It is true he contended on February 7, 1885 and again won at the same location against the Australian Clifford for £1000 and thus gave his compatriots hope that he would also be able to hold his own against Beach in a second match, but this expectation was not fulfilled. On March 28, 1885, he was beaten again by Beach, who now holds the Champion title. ...

October 24, 1885 Hanlan suffered his third defeat on the Hudson. Now it was John Teemer, a young and promising American sculler, who defeated him.

Since Beach doesn't seem to like travelling much, Teemer and Ross will be the heroes of the approaching season. At least they don't have to take the English into account, because on March 10, 1884, Ross defeated the best English rower Bubear from Putney, whom he beat by a whole 10 seconds.

HANLAN STARTED EARLY*

The man who has been responsible, almost wholly responsible, for the great popularity of and for the excellent standing of

Canadians in aquatic sports, is the subject of the sketch, Edward Hanlan. His was a name to conjure with in his rowing days: a name that was known and lauded to the skies from world's end to world's end. No one was anything like a match for him in his palmy days, and no one before or since has ever approached his wonderful record. Edward Hanlan was born of Irish parents in Toronto, July 14, 1855. It is a disputed point as to whether he learned to row or walk first: at any rate, there was but little difference in the time of his accomplishing both tasks. Every spare moment found him with his beloved punt, and it may be hazarded as a guess that he found quite a number of moments for his favourite recreation that were not classed as "spare" by his parents. As mighty oaks from little acorns grow, so did the paddling of the little Hanlan develop into the world-beating sculling of the champion. As in his childhood, he loved poking about in anything bearing the semblance of a boat, so in his youth, he was found beating imaginary opponents on the Bay. It was not long before his shadowy contestants grew into realities, and at the age of 16 he participated in his first real contest. The race was a three-pair affair, in which Hanlan, who rowed bow, with Berry and Duncan as companions, defeated a crew stroke by Pat Gray. In the same year, 1872, he won two singles skull races and he may be said to have begun his career in earnest in that summer. From 1872 until 1896 Hanlon rowed in something like 200 races, and in his aquatic life of twenty-four years, very few decisions were given against him.

During that long period of almost continual matches, it may

---

* *Montreal Daily Herald,* Feb 3, 1900, p.6.

be safely, said that he lost not more than four races through straight out and out rowing; nearly every case in which he pulled second it was the result of an accident.

Beach beat him in Australia, but Beach was so rowed out that he had to be carried from his boat at the end of the race, and this in his own climate and on his own river. Hanlan's active career reads like a fairytale. He has rowed against everybody with any pretensions of sculling ability: he has appeared before all manner of people from the Hawaiians and British Colombian Indians to the elite of London society; from the pauper to the king. He has travelled around the world meeting all comers and journeying halfway around the globe to get matches. His life has been all activity. Nearly 100 of his races have been of the championship variety, and in three matches alone he has won something over $80,000. It is safe to say that, what with match races and exhibitions, of which he has given scores, he has received a direct result of his ability as a sculler $350,000.

FORGED AHEAD RAPIDLY

Hanlan believed in going forward rapidly, and in the year after his debut as a rowing expert, he won the championship of Toronto Bay, beating Williams and McKay. Hitherto he had been racing as an amateur, but in the next year, 1874, he entered upon his professional career, defeating Tom Loudon on Burlington Bay. In 1876, Hanlan rowed in his first foreign race at the semi-Centennial regatta held in Philadelphia, winning three heats in as many days, and cutting the 3-mile record down to 21 minutes nine seconds. At that time, his weight was only 145 pounds. In the same year, he won the championship belt on Toronto Bay by defeating McCann. The next year saw his first defeat, at Boston, as the result of an accident. In that year, too, occurred the first of a series of races, extending over many years against Wallace Ross, the "Black Brunswicker", whom he defeated on Toronto Bay for the championship of Canada over a 5-mile course.

In the following summer, 1878, Hanlan carried off the championship of America by outrowing Evan Morris over the

Hulton course in Pittsburgh. In the same year, he defeated
Charles Courtney for the first of many times. The ensuing
summer saw him in England, carrying the war into Africa in
earnest, for hitherto Englishmen were thought to be unbeatable in
the game of sculls. Hanlin quickly disillusionized the colonies by
winning from Howdon and Elliott, their crack professionals,
within a month of each other. That year saw too, his nearest
approach to a fair defeat, when he rowed a dead heat against
Riley on Kempenfeldt Bay at Barrie. He began his career as an
exhibition scholar in this year, 1879, on his return from England.
In 1879 occurred the unfortunate sawing of Courtney's boat,
when he was matched to row Hanlan at Chatauqua: the latter was
sent over the course alone, and cut down the 5-mile record to 33
minutes 56 $\frac{1}{4}$ seconds, from 35:10. In 1880, the first struggle
against Australia, represented by Trickett, took place over the
Thames course, and Hanlan won, securing the championship of
the world and the cup that went with it. In 1881, he again
vanquished Australia in the person of Laycock, on the Thames,
thus becoming owner of the famous Sportsman's Cup, having
won it three times. On his return from England, Hanlan was
stricken down with typhoid fever, and was obliged to take a rest
for the remainder of the year 1882. In 1883, he beat Kennedy at
Point of Pines, Mass., in a 3-mile race going the distance in 19
minutes, four seconds. In June of the same year, Gaudaur rowed
his first race against Hanlan, together with Teemer and Hosmer.
The result was the usual one. Hanlan won and the next day he
and Lee won the double scull championship over several fast
crews. Hosmer came out in this year. In July, Hanlan beat the
world's record for 4 miles, making it in 27 minutes 57 $\frac{1}{2}$ seconds.
Ten Eyck appeared during this summer.

Stephenson was among the many vanquished in this year,
Hanlan beating him at Vallejo, CA; Lee, too, made his first
attempt against the champion but was hopelessly beaten. In 1884,
Hanlan rowed an exhibition before one of the most cosmopolitan
gatherings probably ever gotten together to see a boat race: the
affair came off at Honolulu, and everybody in the town turned
out— natives, Chinese, Japs, and Americans. From Hawaii, he

went on to Australia, where he defeated Edwards and Laycock, but met his first defeat at the hands of Beach, losing the championship of the world through the interference of the steamer Tonki. On this trip, he defeated Clifford and was beaten, a second time by Beach. On his returning home in 1885, he was accorded a most hearty reception and finished the year by beating Lee, Ross, Hosmer, McKay, and Hamm.

LOWERED THE RECORDS

Hanlan took a shot at the 3-mile record in the next year, and lowered it from 19 minutes 54 seconds, made by Gaudaur, two at 19 minutes 23 seconds at Lake Quinsigamond.

In 1883, he made another excursion to England, but failed in his object – that of getting on another match with Beach. While in the old country, Hanlan tried his hand for the first time stroking a four-oared crew, and succeeded in defeating the English representatives. He spent the remainder of that year on a lecturing tour through England.

In 1887, Hanlan lost the championship of America to Gaudaur at Lake Calumet, Pullman, IL, his boat filling with water. O'Connor rowed his first race against Hanlan during this year at Buffalo. A return match was arranged with Gaudaur, and Hanlan won the championship of America again in very easy fashion.

While making preparations for another trip to Australia, he took on Teemer on the [Toronto] Bay in 1887, and suffered defeat. Arriving in the land of kangaroos, Beach succeeded in winning from him and passed the title over to Kemp, who was also successful in defending it but threw a foul: after defeating Trickett, Hanlan arranged another match with Kemp and lost again through a foul, and in disgust, he left for home. In 1891 Hanlan and O'Connor formed an unbeatable pair, but the growing weakness of the latter, who was labouring even at that time under the fever that carried him off the next year on November 24, put an end to the victorious career, and in 1892 they suffered defeat three times.

In 1893, Gaudaur secured the championship of America again, defeating Hanlan at Orillia.

Hanlan did not row during 1894, and 1895 was spent in coaching the Argonaut crew that did such brilliant work at Henley in that year. He also brought out Toronto University's first crew, which, with a couple months' training under this able master, one the first prize at the Northwestern Amateur regatta at Detroit.

1896 brought him back to his old love, when he defeated Hackett at Rat Portage, Durnan, Rogers, Bubear, and Barry at Belleville, and Hackett again in hollow style at North Bay.

II

RACE ANNOUNCEMENTS
AND REPORTS: 1878-1900
(SELECTIONS)

1878: NORTH AMERICA

ALLEGHENY RIVER, CHAMPIONSHIP OF AMERICA

*No official time was taken, and the reports estimated it all the way from 13.14 to 15.12. On June 20th the race between Hanlan and Evan Morris, of Pittsburg, for the championship of America, five miles, was decided on the Allegheny River, and proved an easy victory for the former. Hanlan's next event was his second match with Wallace Ross, which, after repeated postponements, came off on the Kennebeccasis course on July 31st last. At the first mile stake Ross fell overboard, and left the race a walk over for the Toronto champion. The race was for 1,000 a side, five miles with a turn.

Two weeks after, on August 12th, Hanlan was first in the professional scull race, four miles, $1,000 of the Barrie Regatta Club, rowed on Kempenfeldt Bay...

Lachine was a tremendous feather in Hanlan's cap, and when the American eagle went down under the stroke of his sculls, the whole Dominion of Canada from end to end rang with the sounds of rejoicing. No one there would credit the stories alleging

---

* *Hanlan vs Courtney: A Guide to the Race of 1879* (Buffalo: Baker, Jones & Co., 1879), 21-25.

Courtney's crookedness, for who would buy a race for Ned when he could win it so easily and so certainly?

Charles E. Courtney and Ned Harlan *(1878)*

LACHINE, QUEBEC

*The race, it will be remembered, took place on the 3rd of October, 1878, for a $16,000 purse and 42,000 stakes. All the world was present, and the betting was especially heavy against Courtney, because of the roughness of the water. The morning of the great race opened bright and clear, with a stiff southwest wind blowing, and the water very rough and when the men reached the scene of the race it was still tumbling in a lively manner. Hanlan obtained the choice of position, taking outside to the south, thereby getting the lee of Isle Dorval, the largest island on the course. Mr. Rankin, of the Boston Herald, was appointed judge

---

* Photograph: *Charles E. Courtney / photographed by Ernsberger & Ray. Edward Harlan / photographed by J. Bruce & Co.* United States, 1878. Photograph. https://www.loc. gov/item/94504956/.

Text: *Hanlan vs Courtney: A Guide to the Race of 1879* (Buffalo: Baker, Jones & Co., 1879), 28-39.

for Courtney, Mr. Davis, of Toronto, acting for Hanlan on the boat. Stanley Reynolds, of Rochester, stopped at the turn in Courtney's interest, to see that the buoys were properly rounded. Before the steamer left the buoys the sky to the northwest became completely darkened, lightning began to flash and thunder to roll, and hail and rain to pour, though in the east and over the starting point it continued clear. By the time the steamer returned to the starting point the storm, which was exceedingly violent, had passed over, and the water, which had been very much ruffled, became placid again, the sun coming out in full force and the wind dying away. It was immediately resolved to bring off the race. Meantime train after train had come rushing in, increasing the number of visitors to such an extent that fully ten thousand people had congregated on every point of vantage. It being certain that the race would be run, Sheriff Harding formally announced to the judges appointed by the contestants that he intended to have the race run, and should call out the men by four whistles from the steamer. This occurred about 4:15 P.M., and after waiting some little time, during which Hanlan and Courtney were notified, the steamer proceeded from the dock to a point near the contestants' quarters, where signals to come out were given.

They were obeyed with alacrity, the Canadian champion being the first to make his appearance. He wore a blue shirt with red trimmings, having on his head a red cap. He was followed without delay by his antagonist, who had on a white shirt with a blue star on his breast and a sky-blue cap. Both men as they passed towards the starting point were heartily cheered by the people on the stands and barges on the river. As they approached the press steamer they were eagerly scrutinized. There was a striking contrast between the two men. Hanlan was fair, with clear white skin, while Courtney was dark and tawny as an aboriginal. They were both in splendid condition, their muscles standing out upon their nude arms and legs like huge knots. The Canadian stripped looked like a ***little giant***. With considerable dexterity they wheeled their boats into line, the latter being immediately taken hold of and held by parties stationed at the starting buoys.

A few moments' delay occurred while the judges' barge was being placed in position, after which the referee asked if all were ready. Aye, aye, having been answered by the aquatic heroes, the signal "go" was given.

At 4.56 the men dipped their skulls together and sent the frail shells forward with terrific force, Hanlan making 31 and Courtney 33 strokes to the minute. They appeared to be taking it easily for the first half mile, a waiting race seemingly having been determined on. Up to the first half-mile buoy, no perceptible difference could be discovered. The men were pulling a slow and steady stroke, Courtney especially so. Their style of rowing was somewhat similar, the American being a little jerky as compared with his rival's full, easy and graceful sweep. Before reaching the half-mile signal boat, Hanlan drove the nose of his craft in advance of Courtney's shell. He maintained this position until he passed, when the red flag went up, indicating Hanlan's supremacy so far. Cheers from the Canadians on the press steamer greeted the appearance of their favorite's colors. The next half mile was a repetition of the first, Hanlan making some beautiful and effective sweeps with his skull, still maintaining the lead. The mile was done in seven minutes.

Passing into the second mile the surface of the water was rather more ruffled, in consequence of which both men steered for the lee of Isle Courcelles. When close to the land in calm water Courtney made a determined effort to overhaul his opponent, and succeeding, drew in advance, placing at least a boat's length of daylight between him and Hanlan. The latter had eased off to about twenty-five strokes to the minute, while Courtney made thirty-one. In long, slow strokes they competed for some distance, Courtney slightly increasing his advantage. Kain now began to fall briskly, but did not now last more than a few minutes when it cleared off. As the contestants passed the small speck of land called Dixe's Island, they were again neck and neck in the race, but on approaching the two-mile signal-boat Hanlan drew to the front and passed about a length and a half ahead. Time of the second mile: nine minutes.

At Isle Dorval Courtney rowed a tremendous stroke, steering

straight for the turn buoy, but having diverged very much by getting under the lee of the island, Hanlan obtained a slight advantage and drew almost imperceptibly ahead, turning his rounding buoy in 21 minutes 25 seconds from the start. Courtney was only five seconds behind. Both men lay to their oars, and with great vim strove to obtain the advantage but unsuccessfully. At this time only about a length of the boat and a half separated them, their boats being nearly abreast the press boat which had laid to whilst they passed the buoys. On their return they swept past in magnificent style, each bending to his work with a will and nerved by the cheers of the spectators. The third mile was completed in nine minutes.

Very little change took place in the fourth mile, which was done in six minutes, the men pulling with all their might.

At the commencement of the fifth and last mile Hanlan took the lead, pulling 33 and Courtney 36 to the minute.

Coming down the home stretch some fine skill was displayed, but both men created considerable consternation among the spectators by veering too much south, and rendering it necessary for both to recover ground. Hanlan eventually came in the winner in 36 minutes and 22 seconds.

Before reaching the goal Courtney stopped rowing to avoid a foul, having got into Hanlan's water. 'The latter's time from turning the buoy at two and a half miles, coming downstream, was 14 minutes 50 seconds. The race was adjudged to Hanlan by a length and a quarter.

LACHINE, QUEBEC

*Hanlan was then matched to row five miles against Charles Courtney, of Union Springs, N. Y., for $2,000, considerable interest was manifested in this contest, as Courtney had won numerous races, and was credited with rowing three miles in the

---

* *Edward Hanlan: America's Champion Oarsman*, Wm. E. Harding, the Sporting Editor of the *Police Gazette*, of New York, Richard K. Fox, Publisher, No. 183 William street, New York (New York, 1880).

unprecedented time of 20m. 14$^{1/2}$s. The race was rowed at
Lachine, Canada, on October 3rd, 1878. Thousands of sporting
men from all parts of the United States and Canada assembled to
witness what they anticipated would be a close and exciting
struggle. Large sums were wagered on the race. The betting,
which was at first in favor of Courtney, all of a sudden changed to
$100 to $60 on Hanlan. The race, as far as a contest was
concerned, was a farce. Courtney rowed at a lively pace for two
miles and a half, and then he was no company for Hanlan, who
won as he pleased. After the race, there were numerous rumors
that the race was a fixed up affair, but the truth of the matter is,
Courtney was outrowed and fairly beaten.

After Hanlan had defeated the great overrated Courtney, there
was no oarsman in the United States eager to meet the invincible
Champion, and Hanlan, like Alexander, looked for new worlds to
conquer.

A noted sporting man of Newcastle-on-Tyne, England, was
authorized to match Hanlan against John Hawdon, of Deleval,
England, who was at the time looked upon as the coming
champion oarsman of England. The match was made for £400,
both oarsmen agreeing to row over the Tyne Championship
Course.

At the time the match was arranged, English boating men
both on the Thames and Tyne generally laughed at Hanlan's
ambition in crossing the Atlantic to row Hawdon. And from the
time the match was made the boating men backed Hawdon
heavily, being confident that he would defeat Hanlan. English
boating men little knew that Hawdon was only selected by
Hanlan's backers as a test before he met the best man in England.
After the Canadian began to train on the Tyne every possible
means were taken by his backers to keep the Champion's
advantages, rig and form from Hawdon, but in spite of their
efforts Hawdon's friends became afraid of Hanlan's rig and
refused to bet any amount unless the Hanlan party would give
good odds.

The race was rowed on the Tyne, from the Mansion House to
Scotswood suspension Bridge, on May 8, 1880. Betting was seven

to four on Hanlan, and was pretty freely accepted early in the evening, but later fifty to twenty-five was freely laid. An excellent start was obtained, but the Toronto, bearing Hanlan, soon forged ahead in spite of Hawdon's desperate rowing. Hanlan, with his long sweep, away over his toes, soon gained more and more on Hawdon, with his exhausting thirty-eight to forty-two stroke, with quick recovery, but without much forward reach. When Skinnersburn was reached Hanlan was two lengths ahead. Hawdon was rowing with wonderful energy at thirty-eight strokes to the minute, As the two men sped on towards Redheugh bridge Hawdon had the misfortune to deviate considerably from his correct course. Meanwhile, Hanlan was pulling steadily and looking around to see that there was no danger of his running into any craft that might be ahead of him. He looked composed and sure of victory. Meanwhile the wind, which was blowing downstream, was increasing in force and the water becoming rougher and rougher.

In spite of this disadvantage, Hanlan steadily increased his lead, till it had grown to three lengths. From this point it was evident that he had the race well in hand. He now slowed his stroke from thirty-two to thirty. Hawdon, who was beginning to show signs of exhaustion, also moderated his strokes from thirty-eight to thirty-two. Hawdon was again guilty of bad steering. Hanlan was watching him as a cat does a mouse, and playing with the Tyne oarsman. It was evident now that Hawdon had no chance. The betting was 100 to 1 on Hanlan, barring accidents. The champion's boat flew through the water, keeping well in the middle of the stream. The water was meanwhile breaking over Hanlan's boat, and as he stopped to bail out the water he nodded and laughed to the spectators, who were running alongside the river's edge. The spectators shouted themselves hoarse. This scene occurred when the meadows were reached. Great laughter and fun followed. Poor Hawdon was manfully struggling along, but he was in a piteous plight, thoroughly exhausted. When Cranes was reached Hanlan led by two boat lengths, apparently reducing his lead for the fun of the thing, for he saw that Hawdon was badly out-rowed. Hanlan soon after put on a spurt, and, as he approached the goal, was rowing at 25 to 28.

At Benwell's boat-house Hanlan enjoyed some more laughter, and nodded pleasantly to those on shore. Hurrah! Hurrah! was the deafening cry which was heard at this time. Hanlan bowed and smiled. When Scotswood bridge was reached Hanlan was four lengths ahead, winning by this distance. Cheer after cheer rent the air as he was proclaimed winner. The correct time of the winner is 22 minutes 5 seconds. Hanlan could have beaten Hawdon half a mile if he had wanted to do so.

THE BARRIE RACE

*…comes next in order, as representing the last race in which Hanlan took part, and his virtual defeat. The race was for prizes ranging from $600 down; distance, four miles with a turn. The starters were Elliott, Gaudaur, Kennedy, Riley, Hosmer, Plaisted, Hanlan, McKen, Berry, Jack Hanlan, and Pattullo. The start was a good one.

Hanlan in a very few seconds began to lead, having Plaisted with him and Riley close behind, with Kennedy third and Elliott following. Jack Hanlan put in a heavy spurt and kept well up with his more distinguished rivals. A short time only elapsed till the champion had a good lead, having spurted ahead of Plaisted. He now made for the shore course where the water was better, Riley managing to keep a good place as he had been doing all along; behind these two came Kennedy and Hosmer almost together, the former slightly ahead. Pattullo was ahead of Berry, who had Elliott and Gaudaur in the rear. The turn was made at a time when the position of the judges' boat prevented a good sight of the oarsmen. The champion turned the buoy a little in advance of Riley, who it was plain to see was going to give him a tussle. Kennedy followed third in the turn and the rest of the oarsmen were left almost unnoticed, so intense was the interest of the

---

* *Hanlan vs Courtney: A Guide to the Race of 1879* (Buffalo: Baker, Jones & Co., 1879), 18-45.

onlookers in the struggle between the champion and the Boston oarsman.

The pair did not seem to be putting in their best work, though it was very evident they were by no means playing. Hanlan was pulling thirty-three to Riley's thirty-six, and the third man thirty-three. At the mile buoy, Hanlan led by perhaps a couple of boat lengths. Just here Riley began to spurt and presently the space between the two grew less. Within a couple of hundred yards of the winning buoy the champion wakened up somewhat and began to do better, but Riley settled down more determinedly than ever and kept his position. The excitement at this juncture was intense, and when the judges' gun announced that the first place was taken people were at a loss to know who was the victor.

The two scullers appeared to cross the line at the very same moment and the impression that they had done so was deepened when the second barrel of the gun was discharged, following as the report did as soon after the first as it was possible to make it. It seems as though it was intended to discharge both barrels simultaneously, and that this idea was not a wrong one there is the best reason to believe. Not one of the spectators knew positively which had won. The judges were divided in their opinion, and the referee decided that it was a tie. Kennedy took the next place. Elliott came in followed by Plaisted and Gaudaur. The astonishing time of 17.02 was made, but the measurement was afterwards found to be incorrect.

THE SILVER LAKE RACE, JULY 10

The race at Silver Lake, Wyoming County, N. Y., on July 10th, in which Courtney, the loser of the Lachine race easily beat Riley, the winner of Barrie, serves as a sort of connecting link between those two races, and in connection with them, the straws which show to some extent how the Chautauqua Lake wind blows. In Lachine, Barrie and Silver Lake, the three oarsmen each appear as a winner and each as a loser. The race was a five-miler, with turn, for $500. Rough water prevented the race from coming off during the day, but just before sunset the men appeared, though the water was far from being in a good condition. When the signal was given Courtney's oars were in the water on the instant, the gleam coming from the wet blades like a flash of lightning, but Riley quickly pulled in ahead and began the long lead which embraced so large a portion of the course. But Courtney turned not a hair at thus falling into the rear. Thirty-two strokes to the minute were enough for him, while Riley pulled thirty-six. Two, three and at the half, four lengths behind his antagonist, but this did not seem to cause much trouble in Courtney's mind, though now his strokes began to tell, and his shell narrowed up the gap without any seeming special exertion on his part. As the nose of his boat began to overlap the stern of the other there was a just appreciable spurt on the part of both of the contestants. Prow and stern, prow and thole pins and finally prow and prow, the two boats struggled side by side up the dancing water. Both rowers had sought the lee shore, though it was lengthening out their course to a considerable extent, and they were a little too far from the spectators but going nicely with respect to one another and both pulling in excellent form, and now they were doing all they knew how, and Riley again took the lead and again fell back. They appeared to reach the turning point at about the same time, but Courtney turned with a wonderful celerity and was two lengths away when Riley had got about. Riley halved this gap and they kept down the home-stretch about a length apart.

Both were pulling slowly, Riley twenty-four to the minute and Courtney twenty, but their strokes were giant ones, and the light shells groaned beneath the pressure. Just before coming in Riley gave a valiant spurt and urged his boat to within half a length of the other, but to no avail.

HANLAN AND HAWDON

Following Hanlan to England, we find ourselves upon a triumphant march. His first bout was with Hawdon, an antagonist of no mean calibre, and the way he played with him was the height of enjoyment to his Canadian friends; the depth of aggravation to the simon pure John Bulls. It will be remembered

that Hanlan won the toss for position and took the north side, which gave him shelter for the first half mile. Before the start five to two was offered and taken on Hanlan, but only to a limited extent. At a little before two o'clock the men took their positions at the stakeboats. At the first attempt they started by mutual consent. At the end of the first hundred yards Hanlan had drawn a length ahead and a little further on was fully a length clear, with ease improving his position.

Before the end of the first quarter mile it was felt he was going to be an easy winner, notwithstanding the fact that Hawdon was rowing fast and well. At Skinner Burn, Hanlan was two lengths ahead. He frequently looked around over his shoulder to see that the course was clear, apparently not exerting himself to his fullest powers and seeming quite at ease, as if confident of the result. Approaching Redheugh bridge Hawdon put on a spurt, but it had no effect. Hanlan also quickened up and passed under the bridge with a lead of about three lengths. Hawdon struggled manfully and rowed well and fast, while his opponent continued his easy, quiet style, never apparently exerting himself. After parsing under the bridge the Canadian actually ceased rowing. He allowed Hawdon to draw up almost on a level with him and then with a few strong strokes drew away and resumed his lead of nearly three lengths. The race was from the very first a one-sided affair, although Hawdon rowed gamely. More than once Hanlan allowed the Tynesider to draw up, but with the greatest ease quickly resumed the lead, while every few strokes he looked round to see his course. Near the top of King's Meadow, the men were both in very rough water. Hanlan ceased rowing, and Hawdon with half a dozen strokes pulled up on a level with him. Hanlan smiled and nodded to his pilot, who was following in a cutter, and at once drew away. A little further on Hanlan, to the amusement and astonishment of many, stopped rowing, sponged the water out of his boat, and then setting quickly to work again drew away with ease, and this he did two or three times. He eventually went in the easiest of winners by five lengths and could have won by any distance he liked. His time was twenty-two minutes five seconds. Such a race was never seen on the Tyne. Hawdon is acknowledged to be a capital sculler, and his easy defeat shows what the Canadian can do. At the end of the race Hanlan rowed up to Hawdon and heartily shook hands with him amidst great cheering. Hanlan scaled one hundred and fifty-three and Hawdon one hundred and fifty-two pounds. The Canadian doubtless anticipated a more difficult task or he would not have started at so hot a pace.

THE ELLIOTT MATCH

But if Hanlan aggravated the English by his treatment of their man Hawdon, he won their hearts completely by the artistic way in which he conquered their champion of three seasons. The match was for the honors of championship, together with a purse of £2,000 and the Sportsmen's Challenge Cup. The weather was fine and the water beautifully smooth. Not less than twenty steamers followed the race, and all of them were heavily laden with passengers. Five to one on Hanlan had been laid during the morning, but he came into much better favor just prior to the start, and only a slight shade of odds was laid on the Canadian. Elliott won the toss and took the northern shore.

At 12:15 the men got off to a capital start. Hanlan quickly drew in ahead, rowing very fast, and taking a lead of a quarter of a length, but Elliott spurted gallantly up and reached an equal position. This was, however, the only advantage Elliott had during the race. Hanlan at starting did not display the same nonchalance as when opposed to Hawdon, but as soon as he noticed Elliott was ready he dashed in his sculls with hearty good will. Nothing could be cleaner and more workmanlike than the way in which he obtained a firm preliminary grip of the water and pulled the stroke right through. Elliott was immediately at work with all his might, but buried his sculls too deeply and was unable to recover neatly and promptly. In the course of twenty yards Hanlan had obtained a distinct advantage. But a short distance was traversed when it became evident that Hanlan was destined to have matters pretty well his own way. He sculled with grace and finish, recovering like lightning, keeping his boat on an even keel and seeming to almost lift her out of the water at every stroke. Elliott rocked slightly, splashed frequently and seemed to be exerting his enormous strength to the fullest to little purpose. He persistently demonstrated he was not a master of the new style of using the sculls. Soon after starting, Hanlan deviated somewhat but recovered himself with a clever stroke. After passing Redheugh bridge Elliott spurted with all his power. It was evident he had a tendency to break into his old short, vigorous stroke and was hampered by the new style. The spurt was unavailing. Hanlan had now fallen into a long, telling pull of thirty-six, and Elliott began once more to splash as he did at the commencement of the race. He paused briefly off Lead Works quay to discover his opponent's position, then pulled manfully, evidently relying on his noted staying powers, but the effort was unavailing, Hanlan having off Cooper's Stairs rather increased his lead. At Quay Corner Hanlan was rowing at thirty-four and looking around with great *sang froid*. After the first mile, Hanlan seeing he had the race in his hands, slowed down to thirty-two. Elliott, observing this, by a vigorous effort drew up to within three yards amidst enthusiastic applause. Hanlan slightly increased his pace and kept just ahead, but again eased at Armstrong's, when Elliott came within two lengths of him. Hanlan here almost stopped rowing and turned around to look ahead, although Elliott was still pulling gamely at the rate of thirty-four. The island of King's Meadow was covered by an excited crowd, who seeing the scullers pass in close proximity enthusiastically encouraged Elliott. At the head of the Meadows Hanlan passed to the front and treated Elliott to the backwash of his boat, but Elliott worked away to avoid this annoyance and still spurted pluckily. When off Benwell's boat-house Hanlan stopped rowing to look around to ascertain the distance he had yet to row. About this time a death-like silence fell on the assembled thousands, for England's champion had been defeated almost without an effort. After smiling pleasantly to those on shore, Hanlan began rowing with all his might. The gap between him and Elliott was soon increased, and amid deafening plaudits, Hanlan rowed under Scottswood bridge.

1879: TYNE AT NEWCASTLE

*June 16, Elliott vs Hanlan, Tyne at Newcastle**

Never before were the Tyne's banks so crowded, on the occasion of an aquatic contest, with interested spectators, as on the morning of the 16th of June last, when Hanlan and Elliott contended for the Sportsman's Cup and the Championship of England. Long before daybreak the sport-loving people of Newcastle and vicinity had taken their stations, where each for himself expected to witness the most interesting features of the contest. As the day advanced, trains from all directions deposited their living freight by thousands, and all the avenues leading to the river, or commanding a view of the course were blocked with dense masses of spectators, while every available steamer, and every species of floating craft crowded with visitors, made the navigation of the river a somewhat difficult affair. Both men were in rare trim for the contest, and both were equally confident of success. The odds which had all along been largely in favour of Hanlan grew less and less as the hour for the race arrived, the Tynesiders betting freely in small sums on their champion, whom they believed invincible. A little after twelve o'clock the contestants took their places, and shortly afterwards a fair start

---

* W.H.C. Kerr, *Hanlan's Record: an epic poem* (Toronto: Belfords Clarke & Co., 1879), 14-16.

was made and the race began. Hanlan's bark Toronto led the way from start to finish. He pulled that same strong and long stroke which has so often deceived his opponent and decided the contest in his favour. Rowing ahead, as is his wont, he eased off from time to time until Elliott's craft lessened the distance between them, and then with a few powerful strokes drew quickly ahead. Elliott rowed in magnificent form, and struggled manfully to the close. But it was all in vain.

Hanlan won by eleven boat lengths, the course having been rowed over in 55 seconds less than the fastest time on record. The victory was a decisive one, and with that generous spirit which animates the British nation the Canadian victor was everywhere received with enthusiasm. In its graphic account of the race, the Newcastle Chronicle concludes as follows:

"Our best sculler has been beaten by a better man, and we must be content with rejoicing at the fact that the conqueror, although born beyond the Atlantic, is of the same race as ourselves, and is a citizen of the same vast Empire. Canada has reason to be 'proud of her boy,' and we doubt not that people of the New Dominion will realize the full significance of the victory that their representative sculler has achieved, and will rejoice accordingly."

ELLIOTT VS. HANLAN: JUNE 13, 1879

*While Hanlan was training to row Hawdon, Mr. Renwick published a challenge offering to match an unknown to row William Elliott, the English champion of Great Britain, for £200, and agreed to be present at the Beehive, Newcastle, at an appointed time to arrange the match. Both parties met at Chris Barrass Beehive Inn, Newcastle. Joseph J. Walton, sporting editor of the Newcastle Chronicle, was voted to the chair, on taking which he addressed the meeting at length, saying he considered the most judicious and straightforward way of getting to business was for Mr. Renwick to name his man at once. A discussion

---

* *Edward Hanlan: America's Champion Oarsman* (New York, 1880).

ensued, the result of which was that Mr. Renwick said he would bind himself to limit his choice of a sculler to Robert Watson Boyd of Gateshead or Edward Hanlan of Toronto. Preliminary articles were then and there signed.

At the second meeting, May 5, at Brownlees Oxford Back Bar, Clothmarket, Newcastle, Mr. Whitefoot of the Sportsman presided, and among the company were Colonel Shaw, Mr. J. Davis, Mr. C. J. Starling, and Mr. Samuel Wallace, who represented Hanlan. There were also present W. Elliott, champion; James Taylor, Mr. Richard Thompson, Mr. Chris Barrass, Mr. Brownlee, Mr. Richard Renwick, Mr. George Peel, Wallace Ross, F. A. Plaisted, Mr. Jonathan Cooke. Mr. Renwick named Edward Hanlan as the unknown to row Elliott. After much discussion about a match between Hanlan and Wallace Ross, which finally ended in all parties agreeing that a race between the two provincials ought more properly to be rowed in America, and in Mr. E. Sterling, one of Hanlan's backers, offering to stake $5000 to $4000 for a race between the two on Toronto Bay after their return to America, the...

ARTICLES OF AGREEMENT. Newcastle, May 5, 1879

The draughting of the articles supplementary to those already in existence, which had been interrupted, was then proceeded with, and without the slightest semblance of dispute the following code was agreed to, Colonel Shaw intimating that if the state of the weather should render compulsory an adjournment from the day originally fixed he would pay all expenses:
Newcastle, May 5, 1879.

Articles of Agreement
entered into this day between Edward Hanlan of Toronto, Canada, and William Elliott, of Blyth, to row a straightaway, scullers race over the Tyne championship course from the High Level bridge to Scotswood suspension bridge, in best-and-best boats, for the sum of

£200 a side and the championship of England, together with the challenge cup presented for competition by the proprietors of the Sportsman newspaper. The match shall be rowed on June 16, 1870, one hour and a half before high water on the afternoon tide, according to the A. B. C. tide-table. The scullers shall start from two boats moored twenty-five yards apart, the said boats to be moored to the satisfaction of the referee before the toss for choice for stations takes place. The race shall be rowed under the provisions of the rules laid down for the petitions for the Sportsman challenge cup, and according to such of the new Thames rules of boat-racing as are applicable. The scullers shall start by mutual consent, but if they do not start within fifteen minutes of the time above fixed the referee shall start them by signal or otherwise. The first deposit of £100 a side is now down in the hands of the sporting editor of the Newcastle *Chronicle*, who is hereby named final stakeholder in this match. The second and final deposit of £100 a side shall be made good at the house of Mr. Christopher Barrass, Beehive Hotel, Newcastle, between the hours of 7 and 9 p.m. on Friday, June 13, 1879. The referee shall be chosen at the final deposit, but if the authorized parties cannot agree upon a referee, the representatives of the stakeholder and of the Sportsman shall toss for power of nominating one.

The referee shall have entire jurisdiction over the race from the start to finish, and his decision shall be final, and subject to no appeal at law or otherwise. The referee shall have power to postpone the match from day to day, should he consider that the state of the wind and water will not permit the race to be rowed with fairness and safety to both parties,

Cutters are to be allowed in attendance upon the scullers. Either of the parties to these articles failing to comply with the conditions herein contained, or any of them, shall forfeit the whole of the money deposited.

° (Signed)

Richard RENWICK, William ELLIOTT

Witness to the signatures, Joseph James Walton.

At the close of the meeting, £500 to £400, £1000 to £800, and various other sums were offered on Hanlan, who was a strong favorite. Bets on him were made at £60 to £40 and £5 to £20. During the meeting, Christopher Barrass offered to back Robert Boyd to row Ross on the Tyne for from £100 to £500 a side. Ross declined this challenge. Hanlan, after a tour through Scotland, returned to his old training quarters, and went through a regular routine of training for the race. The final deposit was made in accordance with the articles of agreement, and the final arrangements made.

THE TYNE COURSE

The course, measured in the centre of the channel, is 3 miles and 760 yards, but by keeping well to the north shore, this may be reduced about 30 or 40 yards. The start was from the Mansion House, 150 yards above the High Level bridge, leaving the distance to be covered 3 miles and 570 yards. The course is comparatively straight. The river inclines southward from the High Level bridge, and just above Low Elswickone and three-quarter miles from the bridge, it curves gradually, and takes a slightly northward direction. The great blemishes of the course are the jong gangways of the Tyne General Ferry Company, which run far out into the river, and to avoid which and the steamboat landing stages scullers have to veer out from the north shore into mid-channel. Such maneuvers being rendered necessary imminent risk of fouling are run. The man having the outside station naturally keeps as close as he can to the north shore, without venturing into his opponents water, with the object of shortening his journey, and can scarcely be expected to be able always to divine when his antagonist may choose to begin pulling out so as to row clear of the gangways.

Many fouls have occurred at these spots, and on various occasions the umpire has had the greatest difficulty in deciding which to blame. In other respects the Tyne course possesses many merits. However, it is more exposed than the Thames, and a comparatively slight wind from certain quarters renders it very choppy. At the High Level bridge the width of the channel is about 600 feet. Then it begins gradually to wider till Grindstone quay is reached, then gradually contracts, and off Coopers stairs is very little wider than at the High Level bridge. From this point the channel expands very considerably, until at Low Elswick it is nearly 1,200 feet across. Two and a half furlongs further on the bottom of a long, narrow island, precisely in mid-river, is reached, This obstruction, known as Kings Meadows, is three-quarters of a mile in length, and on either side the channel is rather less than 300 feet wide at the narrowest part. From the top of the Kings Meadows the breadth of the channel is about 700 feet. This is a capital stretch of water, though the banks on either side, being remarkably low and bare, afford no protection whatever from the wind. From the High Level bridge the scullers have a nearly straight run of five furlongs to the Lead Works.

Then comes a bend in the river, which is rendered all the more difficult to pass without accidental collisions in consequence of a contrivance known as the coal staith putting out a long way from the shore. For three furlongs the scullers have to manipulate the curve, taking care to avoid the extremely awkward Dunn street gangway, and if they succeeded in reaching Mile point without a mishap, the worst of their perils are over. They then enter upon a capital reach: of water extending right up to the foot of Kings Meadows. Sir William Armstrong's hydraulic crane marks the mile and a half stage of the journey, and the great crane, or, as it is now called, the platform, the two-mile limit. The head of Kings Meadows is two miles and 350 yards from the starting point, but the best landmark for reckoning is the crane at the east end of

Paradise quay, precisely two miles and a half from the High Level bridge. Benwall ferry is 305 yards higher up the river, and thence the scullers coast along Scotswood Haughs right to the Suspension bridge and the end of the course.

WILLIAM ELLIOTT'S ROWING CAREER

SINCE 1875, William Elliott was born at Hay Farm, Northumberland, November 28, 1849. He stands five feet seven and one-half inches in height; untrained he weighs 176 pounds; trained, 167 pounds. He began his rowing car In 1876, when he defeated William Martin, of Blyth, and afterwards J. Hogarth, the champion of the Wear. His third race was with J. Finnegan, who defeated him after a desperate race. In August, 1875, he entered the Manchester and Sanford regatta. He rowed (in the handicap single-scull) race and won the first heat, defeating Cobbett, to whom he conceded five and a half lengths; but in the second series. J. Anderson of Hammersmith, beat him easily. In the final Nicholson and Smith (Biscuits) came together, and the former was the winner. In March, 1877, Elliott had displayed such form and made such fast rowing on the Tyne that he was entered to compete for the championship cup and £200, open to all comers. The race was rowed on the Tyne, distance: 3 miles 713 yards. Robert Watson Boyd won, and Elliott, with Nicholson and Lumsden, were defeated. Elliott's first match of importance was against George Tarryer, of Bermondsey, which he won easily. Having beaten so good a man as the Thamos sculler, who was credited with having rowed from Putney aqueduct to the Ship at Mortlake in the fastest time on record, his, friends became jubilant, consequently they soon cast about for a fresh opponent, and on the Tyne Robert Bagnall, of the Ouseburn, and William Nicholson went down before him.

On March 4th, 1878, Elliott again competed for the champion cup and £200 on the Tyne course, 3 miles 713 yards straightaway, his opponent being William Nicholson. Elliott rowed a grand race, rowing in high wind and rough water, and winning easily. These successes led the Newcastle people to think they had another champion at hand ready to do battle for the championship, which had vanished from their sight by the last defeat of Boyd by Higgins, and there is little doubt at that time they really had got the best man in the north. With commendable spirit they issued the *defi* to the champion, and they also made a match with Thomas, of Hammersmith, to row on May 6th, 1878, for £200. Higgins, who was then champion of England, accepted the challenge to row Elliott, and the match was made. Thus it will be seen that in the short space of five months Elliott had scarcely been out of training, and he had to row four matches. For this most recent event Elliott, after beating Thomas, went home to James Taylor's at Newcastle, when he was sent to Whitley, journeying to the Tyne each day for his rowing exercise. The race took place on the Thames, from Putney to Mortlake, June 6, 1878, for £200 and the championship. The course was four and three-eighth miles. The Tyne boatmen were confident he would win, and £50 to 440 was readily offered by his backers.

On the day of the race Elliott looked big, and did not take so well in the preliminary spin as Higgins, who never appeared in such good trim for a sculling race before, and the offers of 7 to 4 on Elliott, which were then current, found more takers. Elliott gained two lengths on the first mile; then Higgins took the lead, and reached Barnes railway bridge in 20 minutes 13 seconds, Elliott then being 1 minute 13 seconds in the rear, and finally Higgins passed the judge (Mr. Moore, of the London Rowing Club): opposite the ship, a winner by about 600 yards, his time for the whole course being 24 minutes 33 seconds, nearly two minutes before Elliott. There never was a north vs. south struggle in which more money was speculated in Newcastle than on this occasion. The coin was fairly piled on Elliott, until at one time as much as two to one was laid on the Blyth sculler. Book-makers, however, did not tire of accepting the odds, and were enabled to reap a slight profit through telegraphing to Putney to be on at starting price. This might possibly account for the position which Elliott occupied when the race was begun. Immense interest was manifested in the struggle by the inhabitants of the metropolis of the north, and at 3 o'clock on Monday afternoon there could not have been less than 5,000 persons assembled in front of the offices of the Newcastle *Chronicle* to learn the result. The most lively excitement prevailed in the crowd, and as much as 5 to 1 was laid on Elliott by one sanguine individual. When the telegram, Higgins won easily, was exhibited, therefore, the people were perfectly paralyzed, and for a long time they treated the thing as a practical joke. Elliott was not satisfied with his defeat, for he issued the following challenge. William Elliott, of Blyth, will row any south country sculler a match over the Tyne championship course, in two months' time, for £200 a side. Higgins wanted to row on the Thames, and no match was then made.

On August 31st, 1878, Elliott entered the single-scull race at the Thames international regatta, against J. Higgins, and defeated him easily over the Thames championship course; and, with Nicholson, Boyd and Lumsden, won the four-oared championship. After this race Elliott accepted a challenge from Higgins to row for £200 and the championship, and the race took place on February 17th. Elliott was victorious, and since he has held the title of champion. Elliott is a well-formed, muscular athlete, and the fastest oarsman in Great Britain, and boating men both on the Thames and Tyne were confident he could outrow anyone.

The great race was rowed on June 16th, 1879. A tremendous crowd congregated to witness the contest, Elliott's cutter was first seen making its way down towards the High Level, and the crew disembarked at the logs in front of the Mansion House, where Elilott was in waiting. The ten rowers were: Robert Bagnall (bow), J. Croney, W, Simpson, W. Thompson, W. Lakey, T. Sadler, J. Parker, W. Winship, W. Armstrong, and J. Gallon (stroke), W. Taylor (coxswain). Hanlan's ten-oar followed down on the Gateshead side, and she carried his boat the Toronto, the crew proceeding below the High Level to Boyd's boatyard, where the Canadian was ready to meet them. His cutter was manned as follows: H. Kempster, Wrightson Foster, R. Humble, J. Farrer, M.

Cairns, J. Kempster, Alexander Hogarth, W. Wilkie, T. Barnes, and F. A. Plaisted, the American sculler engaged to row Nicholson on the Tyne for £200 rowed the after oar, and J. Greensitt handled the rudder lines.

Among the Americans present were Mr. J. Davis, Windsor, Ontario; Mr. Starling, Belville, Ontario; Mr. John Elliott, Montreal; Mr. J. Duggin, Toronto; Mr. D. Keith, Toronto; Mr. David Walker, Toronto: Mr. McFarren. Toronto. At 11:50 Elliott was seen on the Mansion House Quay almost ready for action, and he looked brimful of confidence. James Percy, Taylor, and Ralph Hepplewhite launched the fragile England upon the waters as tenderly as if he had been a baby, and the Blyth man was not long in getting afloat. His adversary, however, did not embark until nearly ten minutes later, and as both men made their appearance on the river they were repeatedly cheered in the most enthusiastic manner, and Hanlan removed his cap in response, while a band on one of the steamers played "Bonny Pit Lad," in the north countryman's honor. As soon as it was known that Elliott had won the toss for choice of stations, the men proceeded to their stake boats, but the commencement of hostilities was delayed until 14 minutes past 12 o'clock. The greatest excitement prevailed amongst the thousands of visitors on shore and afloat, and the scene was such as is seldom witnessed even on Tyneside, Elliott selected the northern or Newcastle station, and the men began to perform their racing toilets, the English man stripping to the buff, while the Canadian, as on the previous occasion, rowed in a dark blue sleeveless jersey and blue drawers.

THE RACE DAY

All were on the *qui vive* for the start, and there was almost breathless silence while the sterns of the men's boats were being held, Mr. Ward of Toronto, doing duty for Hanlan, and a friend for Elliott, J. Taylor being in the head of the latter's cutter, and Bright in that of Elliott's opponent. Hanlan, who won the toss for stations when he rowed Hawdon, lost on this occasion, although there was little to choose in this respect, as the boats were well out in the centre of the tide, which, owing to the weight of land water, was moving very slowly.

Elliott chose the Newcastle or northern side, and after the Tynesider's boat had once or twice drifted away from his station they got off on pretty even terms. Hostilities had hardly commenced, however, before Elliiott appeared to be going unsteadily; he dug his sculls deeply, and his style already bore unfavorable contrast with that of his opponent, who was rowing in beautiful form, although putting his sculls in at the rate of 42 to the minute against 40 on the part of Elliott. As they ploughed along at this terrific rate the excitement was beyond all description, more especially that for 150 yards or so the Canadian had pot taken more than a lead of half a length, and Eliiotts thousands of admirers on Tyneside began to congratulate themselves that their man was not going to be so easily beaten after all. He, however, was evidently not *au fait* with the long slide and swivel rowlocks; he splashed very much; moreover, he seemed anxious, and, passing Wylies Quay he looked over his right shoulder to see how far Hanlan was in front of him. Finding that the latter was fully a length in advance, he set to work again in the most determined manner, but it was of no avail, for Hanlan, still rowing at 40 strokes to the minute, and Eiliott at the same rate, was still increasing his lead. At the Skinner Burn, there was nearly a length of daylight between the boats, but from that point to the Redheugh Bridge Hanlan was unable to increase the distance, owing, probably, to his deviation from the course slightly, and that Elliott was working his sculls more evenly than when he started. The bridge was reached in 2m. 35s., and both scullers kept well out in mid-stream, neither relaxing the slightest in his efforts. Presently it could be seen that Hanlan had the race in hand, for he was evidently not rowing at his fastest pace, and still improving his position. Between the Lead Works and Cooper's stairs Elliott once got very deep with his left-hand scull, and his boat was almost brought to a standstill, which enabled Hanlan to get further away, and at Halls Quay corner he was four lengths in advance. The American Champion was now rowing with comparative ease, and occasionally he looked over his shoulder to see if all was clear. As they approached the Dunn street gangway Elliott improved very much in style, and he came up a little, the cheers upon the water and on land being of the most deafening kind.

The mile, less 150 yards, was reached in 6 minutes 11$^{1/2}$ seconds from the time of starting, which is considered to be exceedingly fast, and although Hanlan was beginning to show his usual indifference, Elliott strained every nerve to alter the aspect of affairs, the race proceeding in this way to the High Sheer Legs at Armstrongs Works, where Hanlan led by three lengths, rowing 32 strokes to the minute against Elliott's 37. Halfway up the meadows, where there were immense crowds on either side of the river, Hanlan took Elliott's water, and then rowed on in front of him, both in midstream, but from here to the two-mile post the leader improved his position, being as nearly as possible five lengths in advance. The time was 12m. 8s. for the distance, less 150 yards, and, as they were rowing on to the Paradise Quay, Elliott went across into Hanlan's water, but the umpire's boat, which had been a very long way astern all the time, was now shut out from a view of the race by some of the steamboats, and it became impossible to see by how far Hanlan was leading. It was evident, however, that, bar accident, all was over, for Hanlan seemed to be doing just as he pleased; sometimes he appeared to be half a dozen lengths in front, then only half that distance, but he must have considerably increased his lead after passing the ferry above Paradise, for the judge, Mr. Swaddle stated that he had won the race by 11 lengths: Time 21m. 1s., just one minute faster than when Elliott beat Higgins.

Hanlan, after his victory, was pronounced a wonder, and the English press acknowledged him to be the most speedy and finished oarsman that was ever seen on the Thames or Tyne. Hanlan returned to America. He received a grand reception in New York, and Toronto, his home, received him with open arms. Of course, Hanlan was received by his fellow citizens and countrymen in the warmest manner when he came home, after teaching the Englishmen that "Champion of Canada" was a prouder title than "Champion of England."

Hanlan was doomed to meet with something very like a reverse soon after his return to his native city. On the 18th of August, he was foolish enough to start in the professional race at the Barrie Regatta, though he knew very well that he was far from being in condition for anything like a hard contest. His trip to England had certainly done him no good, and he did not improve after his return to Canada as he ought to have done. He was not high in flesh and out of condition in that respect, but on the other hand, he was thin and light enough for a hard race, but at the same time comparatively soft and flabby. Indeed, at this time it was feared by many of his friends that the Champion was breaking up altogether, and that, young as he was, he was already passing into physical decadence. Their great anxiety was to induce him to put on flesh again with the same surprising rapidity that had been his wont in 1878, but it seemed as though this could not be done. For a time he had almost quit rowing and devoted himself as nearly as possible to absolute rest, and it was during this time that he suddenly made up his mind to start at the Barrie Regatta.

In the race there were numerous starters, but the dangerous men were James H. Riley and John O. Kennedy. Hanlan was placed near the outside of the course and Riley more in shore. Now it happened that the scow which constituted the judges stand at the start and finish, had dragged anchor somewhat the night before the race, and as the starting line was an imaginary one drawn from a flag on this scow to one on a corner of one of the piers inshore, the course drawn by Hanlan must have been a length or more longer than Rileys, while the score for start and finish was not at right angles to the course as it was supposed to be.

When the word was given Hanlan struck off at a great rate, and was soon so far ahead that he looked like a sure winner. He lost some time at the turn, however, and as they were on their way home Riley gained upon him rapidly. While they were yet some distance from the finish Riley secured a lap on him, and then Hanlan struck out more vigorously, though he was evidently pretty tired. As he neared the finish Hanlan kept his eye on the inshore flag, and he could sight this easily across the prow of Riley's shell, looking at right angles to the course, he felt sure he had won the race when the gun was fired, but from the scow the judges saw the finish differently and declared it a dead heat. Hanlan declined to row the race off the next day, and first money was accordingly awarded to Riley.

❧ 3 ❧

1879: CHAUTAUQUA LAKE, NY

A Guide to the Great Race of 1879[*]

HOW IT CAME ABOUT

In the great race of 1879 we find an eloquent exemplification of the old maxim, that "two heads are better than one." The problem of getting together two men so proverbially hard to please as Charles E. Courtney and Edward Hanlan had puzzled many brains for a long time. The summer was well nigh spent in a fruitless search for the exact proposition which would suit both the American and the Canadian champions. Offers of the most tempting description were made by the railroads and the hotel men.

James Gordon Bennett bated the Saratoga hook with a large purse. The Canadian courses were not behind-hand in their offers. But all to no avail. One after another these various propositions were snubbed by the giant oarsmen, Whose particular noses got so high in the air that many feared they would never come down. Certain it was that nothing less than a miracle would ever satisfy their high-mightinesses.

---

[*] *Hanlan vs Courtney: A Guide to the Race of 1879* (Buffalo: Baker, Jones & Co., 1879), 2-25.

At length it fell in the way of a certain patent-medicine man of Rochester to snuff a huge advertisement in the Courtney-Hanlan air, and being a man of great shrewdness and foresight, he immediately set about the difficult task of solving the problem which had proved so unanswerable up to that time. A feeler was put forth in the newspapers in the shape of a $5,000 offer, open to all comers, with the championship honors attached, and the promptness with which a negative reply came back to him from Union Springs and Toronto was a touching commentary upon the efficiency and promptitude of Uncle Sam's letter-carriers when bad news is to be brought.

These replies knocked Mr. Soule, the medicine man, as flat as a pancake, and he would probably have retreated ignominiously from the field had not Mr. W. S. Baldwin, a prominent railroad man and editor of Buffalo, smelled the flavor of success in a modification of Mr. Soule's offer, and set about the task of wringing a victory out of the latter's defeat. Scarcely had the ink on the first proposition grown dry, before Mr. Baldwin was in Rochester and button-holing Mr. Soule. The result of this conference was a second offer, which "raised" the first a thousand dollars, omitted the championship business and narrowed down the contest to the two men, Hanlan and Courtney. Then followed a hard two weeks' job for Mr. Baldwin, embracing numerous jaunts to Toronto to confer with the Hanlanites, a vigorous onslaught on the purses of the corporations and citizens of Chautauqua Lake, who must benefit by the race, if it was rowed on their waters, and the difficult task of keeping his secret clear from inquisitive eyes. Suffice it to say he was successful in all that he undertook, to the joy of every lover of the most manly of sports that the world ever looked upon; he won the golden consent which had been so eagerly and so vainly sought in the labyrinth of the two great oarsmen's minds. The one condition which both the boatmen waited for was the freedom to make their own newspapers in the shape of a $5,000 offer, open to all comers, with the championship honors attached, and the promptness with which a negative reply came back to him from Union Springs and

Toronto was a touching commentary upon the efficiency and promptitude of Uncle Sam's letter-carriers when bad news is to be brought.

These replies knocked Mr. Soule, the medicine man, as flat as a pancake, and he would probably have retreated ignominiously from the field had not Mr. W. S. Baldwin, a prominent railroad man and editor of Buffalo, smelled the flavor of success in a modification of Mr. Soule's offer, and set about the task of wringing a victory out of the latter's defeat. Scarcely had the ink on the first proposition grown dry, before Mr. Baldwin was in Rochester and button-holing Mr. Soule. The result of this conference was a second offer, which "raised" the first a thousand dollars, omitted the championship business and narrowed down the contest to the two men, Hanlan and Courtney. Then followed a hard two weeks' job for Mr. Baldwin, embracing numerous jaunts to Toronto to confer with the Hanlanites, a vigorous onslaught on the purses of the corporations and citizens of Chautauqua Lake, who must benefit by the race, if it was rowed on their waters, and the difficult task of keeping his secret clear from inquisitive eyes. Suffice it to say he was successful in all that he undertook, to the joy of every lover of the most manly of sports that the world ever looked upon; he won the golden consent which had been so eagerly and so vainly sought in the labyrinth of the two great oarsmen's minds. The one condition which both the boatmen waited for was the freedom to make their own conditions, and Mr. Baldwin was the first man to see it. His reward cannot fail to be a princely one; and as for Soule—oh, don't we wish that us was him!

Having obtained the consent of the principals to row at a time and place which should be mutually agreeable, it became necessary to hold a meeting for the purpose of arranging the details of the race. This took place at Rochester on the 13th of September, time having been given to the backers of the two men to look into the matter, of course, and make their various plans according to the light of knowledge. Mr. Baldwin, who had the interests of Chautauqua Lake in view, worked very hard, and at the time of coming together it was an understood thing that Mr.

Soule would favor that course, and pocket ten or fifteen thousand dollars thereby.

Courtney and Hanlan, with their backers, reached Rochester the afternoon of the day set for arranging the preliminaries, and as soon as they had worked away the cinders they proceeded to business. A room had been engaged for the conference and hither they were led, the oarsmen meeting each other in the spirit of friendly rivalry. Mr. W. S. Baldwin was present to advocate Chautauqua Lake as the most feasible course, and Messrs. Schell, Parker and Sogers of Geneva came to point out the advantages of their lake. Saratoga and Pittsburgh had no representatives, and it was evident that they had withdrawn on the strength of the correspondence held with the members of the Hanlan Club. Mr. Asa T. Soule was elected chairman, and the business was conducted under his supervision. After reading the rough skeleton of the articles of agreement which had been drawn up on the same model as the Ross-Hanlan contract, which seemed to be satisfactory to all parties, the interested ones withdrew to a private room to discuss the momentous question of the referee. Mr. Courtney stated that there were three men whom he was willing to trust, all of them from New York City: Mr. John Eustice of the old Atlanta crew, Mr. W. E. Curtis of the *Spirit of the Times*, and Mr. William Blaikie of the New York *Herald*. It happened that the last-named gentleman was the first choice of the Hanlan men, so they gracefully agreed to accept his name, providing that he was willing to serve. A special clause was added to the articles of agreement that the referee's expenses should be evenly divided between the contestants. After filling out the blanks in the skeleton, which covered all the points insisted on by the two sides, they were signed and witnessed and read as follows:

ARTICLES OF AGREEMENT: SEPTEMBER 12, 1879

entered into this 12th day of September,
A.D. 1879, between Edward Hanlan of
Toronto, Ontario, and Charles E.

Courtney of Union Springs, N. Y., who hereby agree to row a five-mile race with turn, in best and best boats, in accordance with the following articles:

Article I. —The said race shall be for the sum of six thousand dollars, offered by the Hop Bitters Company of Rochester, said prize to be known and designated as the "Hop Bitters Prize."

Article II. —The said race to be rowed on Chautauqua Lake on the 8th day of October, 1879, between the hours of three and six in the afternoon, smooth water required, subject to the decision of the referee, who is hereby empowered to postpone the race to the next day, or the first favorable day thereafter, if the water is not in fit condition for the race to come off.

Article III.—Said Hop Bitters' Prize of six thousand dollars shall be deposited in the City Bank of Rochester five days- before said race is rowed, and shall be payable on the order of the referee to the winner of said race.

Article IV.—Mr. William Blaikie, of New York, to be referee and his decision to be final. The referee to accompany the men over the course if possible. The contesting parties to share his expenses.

Article V.—The men shall toss for choice of position before starting in the race, and shall be started after preliminary warning by the word "go," said word to be given by the referee. The men shall start from two boats moored twenty-five yards apart, and shall row two and a

half miles to buoys securely anchored and properly marked by flags twenty-five yards apart, each man to turn his own buoy from port to starboard and return to place of starting.

Article VI.—The referee, in case of any outside interference, if it effects the result of the race, shall order the men to row over again on the first favorable day, under the original conditions.

Article VII.—The race is to be governed by the laws of boat-racing, as adopted by the National Association of Amateur Oarsmen, subject, however, to the conditions of these articles.

Article VIII.—Each party has the right to select a judge to look after his interests, who shall be allowed to accompany the referee over the course, and any point of disagreement shall be finally settled by the referee.

Article IX.—A judge for each man shall be chosen by mutual consent to see that the turning buoys are not molested or changed; also a judge for each at the finish, with a referee to decide which crossed the winning line first.

Article X.—It is hereby mutually agreed that all steamers and boats must be under the absolute control of the referee or committee appointed by the referee.

[Signed]

Charles E. COURTNEY, Edward HANLAN.

Witnesses—David SHAW, James H. BRISTER.

Mr. Blaikie was notified by telegraph of his appointment, and replied that he was willing to serve, but in order to insure the fairness of the race the men must agree to abide by these conditions, in the absence of which he was unwilling to identify himself with any race: 'That a line of flags should be placed between the men; that either sculler should be disqualified by two false starts, also for crossing the line; that he should have the privilege of naming a morning hour in case of postponement; that he should have the use of a steam launch capable of making twelve miles an hour; that Hanlan, Courtney and Soule should sign and send a statement that no one in the interest of either contestant should furnish any part of the money to be rowed for. In due time these additional conditions were signed and the great race was a settled thing. It only remained for the contestants to go into training, for the people to get worked up to the proper state of excitement, for the railroads to oil up all their extra rolling stock, and for the king of the Indian Summer to be induced to take a hand in the contest,—something which a Great Medicine Man like Soule ought to have no trouble in doing,—and the success of the great aquatic event had become assured. It now remains for us to see how well the various contracts are filled in this momentous struggle.

A SCARE

Tuesday, Sept. 23rd, had been set apart as the date on which the oarsmen would go to Chautauqua and begin their severe training. The New York *Herald* of the Sunday previous published a disheartening dispatch to the effect that Courtney was in a bad condition, stormy days having made it necessary for him to work at night, and this causing chills and blistered hands. There were no indications, however, that he intended to back out of a race.

But on Tuesday morning a Toronto paper came out with an announcement, which the associated press telegraphed all over the country, that Hanlan was ill, and would not be able to row until spring. This of course occasioned a great deal of talk and considerable disappointment among those who were interested in the race. There were some who believed the report to be a canard, got up for the purpose of offsetting the bad news from Union Springs, but the general opinion was that the race would not come off until 1880. An investigation into the matter showed that Hanlan was really unwell, and his physician declared positively that he could not be got into condition by October 5th. The outcome of the matter was a postponement until October 16th, a step which is satisfactory to all parties concerned. Both men went to Chautauqua on the 25th of September, and it is believed the bracing air of that elevated region will prove medicine to both.

AMERICA'S HOPE: C. E. COURTNEY

It is hard for an American to look upon the towering form of Charles E. Courtney, with broad arched back, splendid shoulders, and tough, knotty muscles, and not believe that the cloud which has rested upon his fair fame since his defeat of October 3rd, 1878, at Lachine, is about to be swept away into the shining light of victory.

It is equally hard to look into his pleasant, manly face and hear his cheering voice, so ringing with friendliness, so open in its utterance, and believe that he ever sold himself and his friends for Canadian money. To know the man is to like him instinctively, for he has many very estimable traits in his composition.

Mr. Courtney can surely claim to be one of the original "Forty-niners," having made his first appearance in this world in that good year. His birthplace is Union Springs, a little village upon the east shore of Lake Cayuga, within a few miles of the City of Ithaca. When only seven years of age the lad Charlie lost his father, and it became necessary for him to earn his own living. He was apprenticed to a carpenter in his native place, and learned how to hit the nail on the head in the various ways which the trade demands. Hard and toilsome was his boyhood according to his own description. Nature had given him a bright head and a love of knowledge; but in the place of books he was forced to spend his boyhood's hours with the saw and the adze and the carpenter's square. But, although he grew up with very little of book-learning, he became a master of his trade, and even now delights in boasting, and not without reason, that he is a much better carpenter than oarsman. Nor did his toilsome childhood prevent the growth of his physical being, and he shot up to his present magnificent proportions, standing six feet, one-half inch in his socks, and weighing, when in condition, from 170 to 172 pounds.

Boating had been the only amusement of his minority. Ever since he was knee high to a grasshopper, the young Courtney was hanging about the various rough craft which came in his way. He took to the oar as naturally as a duck to water, and performed wonderful feats of propulsion, no matter what the means might be, oars, paddles, poles or tin pans. His companions conceived a dislike to racing with his boat, and after he had got possession of one which was capable of anything like good time, he began to measure oars with the amateur champions of the Lake, and always to their sorrow. As soon as he was old enough he went to distant points and took part in innumerable amateur regattas, battling with men who had come to be regarded as well-nigh invincible, and teaching them by rough experience the saying which he has since been so fond of repeating, that "there is no oarsman so fast that he has not a superior somewhere." In short, in the seventy-three races in which he took part before entering the ranks of professional scullers, Courtney was never defeated. The trophies which adorn his home at Union Springs would make a foreign general green with envy. The first important victory achieved by Courtney was the senior sculls, Saratoga regatta, September 11th and 12th, 1874, in which he defeated Yates, Keator and other noted college rowers. August 28th, 1875, he captured the Diamond Medal and Championship of New York State, and such amateur giants as W. B. Curtis, Edward Blake, Frank Yates and David Roche, paid tribute to the power of his biceps and the soundness of his breathing apparatus. In September of the same year he tried a double scull race at Troy, N. Y., with R. A. Robinson, of Union Springs for partner, and added another trophy to his collection. At the Saratoga regatta of the Centennial year, he and Yates easily won the double scull race; and in the same year Courtney's boat came across the line first at Philadelphia.

This contest ended the amateur career of the Union Springs oarsman, whose prowess made him appear a tempting antagonist to James H. Riley, who at that time had made some very excellent turns of speed. He was challenged by the latter, and the terms agreed upon, for a match at Greenwood Lake, New Jersey, to come on July 14, 1877. All the preparations for a meeting were completed, and the men had trained into excellent shape, but a few hours before the time set for the race Courtney was taken violently ill, and his physician declared, to the disappointment of an immense crowd of people, that he would not be allowed to row for some time. The race was postponed until August 28th, and the place was afterwards changed to Saratoga Lake, where the American champion had won so many victories. Here he came to the scratch grandly, and with Riley and Bob Plaisted for opponents, reeled off his little three miles with a turn in 20 min. 47$^{3/4}$ sec. Although winning a purse and stake of $800, the hero won a name of far greater value to him. One of the chief promoters of this race was John Morrisey, to whom more than any other man is due Saratoga's chance for its connection with so many brilliant records with the shell and oar. It was the last boating contest ever identified in any way with the name of Senator John.

Courtney's next race was held upon Owasco Lake for a large sum of money and the championship of the United States. The distance was three miles with a turn; and in the race against Courtney were Riley, "Frenchy" Johnson, the colored oarsman, (who is one of Courtney's trainers in the coming contest at Chautauqua) Lake, Ten Eyck, Laberger and others. The race came off September 27th. A good start was made at 5:09 P.M. Courtney took lead from start and held it to close, Johnson second to the mile and a half stake boat, with Riley third. On the return, Riley passed Johnson in the first quarter mile and lapping Courtney, rowed a most exciting race for nearly half a mile. He never changed his long powerful stroke, and on the last quarter

led Riley gradually and easily, and came in at the finish a length and half ahead. Courtney won in 21:29$^{1/2}$, Riley came in second in 21:33$^{3/4}$, Johnson in 21:42, and Ten Eyck in 21:43$^{1/4}$. The remaining oarsmen strung along, several seconds later.

Ill luck did not strike Courtney until 1878, the beginning of defeat being an incurable cold, caused by an upset in a race upon Seneca Lake with James Dempsey. This occurred in June, but the following Fourth of July, Courtney again measured oars with Dempsey at Skaneateles Lake, and showed that worthy that though perhaps Courtney might get beaten in the water, he could not be passed in a boat; at least not by the Dempsey muscle. On the 35th of August he very foolishly took part in an open regatta on Silver Lake, Plympton, Mass, while suffering from indisposition, and the result of this act—a piece of foolhardiness on his part, considering the fact that negotiations were then pending for a race with the Toronto champion, Edward Hanlan, and Courtney knew his friends would bet their bottom dollar on that race. The result of the Silver Lake foolishness was a disastrous defeat of Courtney by "Frenchy" Johnson and others of lesser note. Then came Lachine, the darkest page upon the life's volume of Charles E. Courtney. We give no description of their race here, as it is fully outlined in another chapter.

The question of Courtney's honesty in the matter is still unsettled, but it is safe to say that those who know him best are now satisfied that his honor was not left behind in that unfortunate contest. Many who went against him in the first agony of their depleted purses, have since taken back the harsh things they said about him; and many more who vowed they would never support him again will back his name with their bottom dollar this year—and win. Without wishing to put himself forward, the writer is fair to say that the facts in the case since the day when the red flag of Canada went above his colors, have been very much in his favor. The indignation with which he sold all his boats and turned his back upon them, not to be drawn back save at the earnest solicitation of friends, was that of an honest man. In fact, all his conduct since then has been a good many degrees above par. As for the money he would have made had he sold the race, it has never appeared. But there is another fact which ought to weigh heavily in the evidence and that is the fact that the leading men of the Hanlan Club are gentlemen in every sense of the word, and we have it from their mouths that the accusations against Courtney—and equally against them were not possessed of a shadow of a truth. In this connection it will perhaps be well to state a pertinent fact or two, and give a bit of seasonable, though perhaps unwelcome, advice, to the friends of Courtney, the newspapers, and the American public generally.

One of the greatest secrets in the tremendous chain of successes which have been wrought by Edward Hanlan, lies in the existence of the Hanlan Club. This little knot of friends have formed a cordon about the Canadian champion, and hold him a prisoner, allowing no rays to fall upon him but those of enthusiasm and unbounded faith. Everything in the life of the man is kept rose-colored to his eyes. His troubles are borne by other shoulders. He is not allowed to think for himself or do for himself. The one thing which is impressed upon his mind is his own infallibility, and he goes into a race without a tremor. Result: unshaken nerves, and muscles steeled by that wonderful power—*Confidence*,—in other words. Victory!

On the other hand, Courtney's friends are doubters. With sensibilities far more keen than those of Toronto's darling, he is allowed to catch every whispering rumor which goes about concerning him. Imagine the effect of his backers at Owasco Lake approaching him at the last moment and saying: "Now, Charlie, do your best, for I have staked a great deal upon you in this race." Or imagine the effect at Lachine just before the race, of the *Herald*'s correspondent coming to him and saying: "Courtney, what's this rumor about your selling the race?" It is such fooling as this which makes men lose the race. Handicap Sleepy Tom— grandest of pacers—with a driver who does not pet and talk to him continuously, and the blind horse falls far below his record.

Handicap Charles E. Courtney—greatest of oarsmen, the king who should be invincible—with cowardly backers and still more cowardly rumors, started doubtless by his enemies, and you are sure to have him realize your worst fears! This, dear friends, is somewhat out of the line of biographical detail, but it is something well worthy of consideration. After the Lachine catastrophy Courtney could not be induced to touch an oar for a long time, though many believed him capable of beating Hanlan under favorable conditions. But the honors won by his great antagonist in England aroused the lion within him, and, backed by promises of renewed faith from many of his friends, he bought back his shell and got his hands upon the beloved oars once more. He established a private course on Cayuga Lake, with landmarks which enabled him to time himself accurately, though no observer could tell how fast he was going; and whenever the telegraph reported any very fast time, he set to work and did not rest until he had beaten it. Fortunate would we be if we could record some of the records which he has made in secret, and which he will divulge to no man!

July 15th, of the present year (1879), witnessed a contest between Courtney and Riley, on Silver Lake, in Wyoming County, N. Y. The race was rowed under adverse circumstances; the water was rough; the course was not a certain one in measurement; Courtney was not in racing condition, tipping the scales at $188^{1/2}$; and the time, which was marvellous, if correct, being 27 min. $37^{3/4}$ sec., had to be taken from the stopwatch held between Courtney's feet. He was an easy winner, however, whatever the distance or time; and Riley's subsequent work when pitted against Hanlan makes the prospect for Courtney in the coming contest very favorable, though, of course, these races cannot be made criterions of the meeting at Mayville.

Courtney's last public appearance was an exhibition race at Charlotte, in which he beat "Frenchy" Johnson by half a length with little effort, in 22.05. In rowing Courtney takes a very long, easy stroke, dipping his oars deep into the water, and fairly lifting his boat at every dip. It has been said of him that he never spurts, though the "Pinafore" joke might be applied with truth in this instance. In his own language, however, he does not believe in spurts, but in slow, steady, unremitting pounding, doing his level best every time he puts his blades into the water. He has unbounded resources in the way of wind, and the long distance to be rowed at Chautauqua Lake is very much in his favor.

But the present year (1879) has been the crowning one in Hanlan's career, and though many believe his star has ceased to be in the ascendant since Riley took the Barrie money away with him, it did not begin to fall until he had reached the zenith of fame, and left the English speaking world—which means the world of oarsmen—in the wake of his gallant shell. His victories in English waters are still fresh in the minds of our readers.

On the 5th of May, he fairly played with Howdon at Newcastle-on-Tyne, stopping several times to bail out his boat and taking things very easy generally.

June 16th he had another day's sport with Elliott, who had three times won the championship of England, and aggravated his victory by almost ceasing to row as he turned to look ahead. The course in this race was a little short and the time is of no value. At Barrie, Hanlan and Riley were adjudged a tie, but the champion refused to row it over again, and the prize was given to the Boston man. The time in this race, four miles with a turn, was 17.02, but it is almost universally conceded now that the course was not full measurement.

Hanlan is without doubt one of the most finished scullers in the world—a master in the art who performs no botched work. His slide is exceptionally long, and he makes use of every inch of it, the result of which is a long, sweeping stroke beautiful to look upon and terrible in effect. In steering he is without an equal, and rough water, the bane of most oarsmen, gives him a marked advantage in a race. Hanlan is five feet eight and three-fourths inches in height. He is slightly gaining in weight, his fighting number in 1878 being 152 lbs. and in 1879, 153.

THE REFEREE: All lovers of fair play and honest racing have reason to felicitate themselves in the choice and acceptance of

William Blaikie to the responsible and difficult position of referee for the Mayville match. Mr. Blaikie is a New York lawyer of undoubted honesty and unquestioned capability. He was a capital oarsman in his college days, having been with the Harvard crew when Yale and Harvard were the only crews worth talking about, and before Columbia, breathing the same air as Courtney, and catching the infection of his prowess from the waters of Cayuga Lake, had taken the aquatic honors of the colleges into the Empire State. And ever since leaving college Mr. Blaikie has kept in the advance rank of the worshipers of the oar, loving it because he believed it the best possible means of physical culture and not as a means for gambling. He is sternly opposed to all forms of betting, and never could be prevailed upon to act as referee in a race in which the contestants put up money. Moreover, Mr. Blaikie is a strict disciplinarian. Quick to discern, prompt to stop any tricky rowing, he will be quite certain to insure a fair race. In fact his codicil to the articles of agreement, printed in another chapter, will do much to render it a sure thing.

THE COURSE: As will be seen by the accompanying map, the course selected as the one best fitted for the coming contest, begins not far from the steamboat wharf at the Mayville end of the lake, and runs in a south-easterly direction towards Long Point. It will be plainly marked on the day of the race by a line of Hags, the oarsmen being obliged to keep on the side first drawn, and any attempt to cross being adjudged a foul. This line will be two and a half miles in length according to the articles of agreement, and the final measurement which will be made by Mr. Blaikie in person, will ensure the honesty of the distance and the correctness of the time taken. The public may rest assured that Mr. Blaikie will make no mistake.

We are indebted to Mr. Baldwin, the popular passenger agent of the Buffalo, Chautauqua Lake and Pittsburgh Railroad, for his excellent map of the lake and the course as it has been marked out. The new Extension Railway, now in process of construction, will run within a few rods of the latter for its entire length.

THE GREAT SINGLE SCULL RACE BETWEEN

HANLAN AND COURTNEY

For the "Hop Bitters" Prize of $6,000, on

CHAUTAUQUA LAKE,

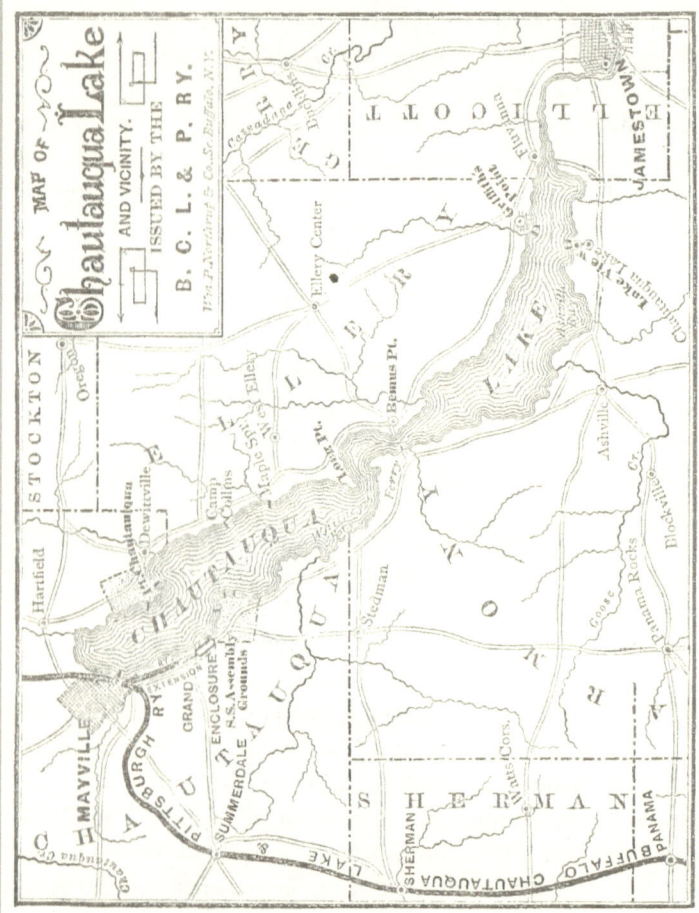

THURSDAY, OCTOBER 16th, 1879,

WILL BE ROWED NEAR MAYVILLE, AT THE HEAD OF THE LAKE.

Tickets and full information on application to

J. A. BURCH,   W. S. BALDWIN,
Gen. East'n Pass. Agt. L. S. & M. S R'y,   Gen. Pass. Agt. B., C. L. & P. R'y,
Buffalo, N. Y.   Buffalo, N. Y.

1880: CHAUTAUQUA LAKE, NY AND NEWCASTLE

CHAUTAUQUA LAKE: MAY 18, 1880

*Hanlan's next appearance in public was at Chautauqua Lake, where he was to row Courtney a race of five miles with turn for a purse of $6,000. The circumstances attending this attempt at a race did much to weaken the hold which aquatics had taken upon the esteem of the Canadian people. The whole truth of the case may never come out, but this much is pretty certain: Courtney was funking and did not want to start unless the race could be fixed for him to win. Hanlan's friends promised that he would be allowed to win, without any intention of keeping to their agreement. In other words, they proposed meeting fraud with fraud, making Courtney's supporters, and not Hanlan's, the victims. On the day before the race one of Ward's most intimate friends made a play or pay bet of $1,000 on Hanlan to $700 on Courtney. The thing was done very quietly, and the man who backed Courtney was a total stranger to the Canadian party. Unfortunately for the little game that was being played, however, the stranger was only betting $200 of his own money, the other

---

* *Edward Hanlan: America's Champion Oarsman*, Wm. E. Harding, the Sporting Editor of the *Police Gazette*, of New York, Richard K. Fox, Publisher, No. 183 William street, New York (New York, 1880), 19-28.

$500 being put up for Courtney's friend and adviser, J. H. Brister.
When Brister learned the name of the gentleman who had put up
the $1,000, he knew that he and the rest of the Courtney party
were getting what is known in sporting parlance as the double
cross. That evening Courtney's boats were sawed; and very few
are now found who doubt that the sawing was done with the
knowledge and consent of both Brister and Courtney. This closed
the season of 1879 so far as Hanlan is concerned.

On the 19th of May, 1880, Hanlan defeated Courtney with
ridiculous ease on the Potomac at Washington, and on the 26th of
the same month he defeated Riley over the same course, without
ever being compelled to exert himself. A few weeks later Hanlan
rowed in the regatta at Providence, R.I., June, 1880.

The distance was four miles with a turn.

The following started: Wallace Ross, St. John, N. B.; Geo.
W. Lee, Newark, N.J.; James H. Riley, Saratoga, N. Y.;
Horatio Delano, Chelsea, Mass.; James A. Ten Eyck,
Peekskill, N. Y.; F. A. Plaisted, Boston, Mass.; Jacob
Gaudaur, Toronto, Can.; Jas. H. Dempsey, Geneva, N. Y.;
R. W. Boyd, Middlesbro, Eng.; Edward Hanlan, Toronto,
Can.
Of those who had entered the following withdrew:
John A. Kennedy, Geo. W. Weisgerber, Frenchy Johnson,
and G. H. Hosmer.

Not within our recollection were so many high-class scullers
previously started in a race, and the stillness which fell upon the
vast throng, and the eager intensity of their gaze as the men sat
with oars poised and teeth set awaiting the signal, showed how
deeply concerned all were in the contest between these giants of
the oar. All eyes were fixed on Hanlan and his next-door neighbor,
Boyd, and when it was noticed that the champion began at once
to draw away from the Englishman, the manifestations of
satisfaction were unmistakable. Fast as Hanlan went, however,
Plaisted traveled still faster, jumping away with the lead, but he
was early called upon to resign it to Ross, who was putting in long,

powerful strokes, which proved more than Fred could withstand, and he quietly fell back to fourth place as Riley dashed past after Ross, who at the three-quarters was a little in advance of Hanlan.

For a mile and a half the race between Ross, Hanlan and Riley was terrific, but the former's vigorous stroke had by that time forced him almost a length ahead not much to gain ordinarily in that distance, but a lot for anybody to snatch from the champion. At this time the fourth man was Gaudaur, and he was followed by Dempsey, Lee, Ten Eyck, Plaisted, Boyd, and Delano, the fast work done by Plaisted and Boyd at the start having tired them badly, and thus sent them to the rear. About a quarter of a mile from the turn Hanlan, who had been rowing in front of Riley, was observed to cease pulling long enough to lose several strokes, and when he resumed he did not put the life characteristic of him into his work, and Riley managed to get around his stake ahead of the Canadian, who seemed to be in difficulties from some cause. Ross turned both his own buoy and the one next to it, by which he didn't gain anything, although, as the sequel proved, he didn't need more than he already had to make his election sure. He had pulled a magnificent race so far, and the pace all the way very fast, faster than the New Brunswick sculler had ever before carried an opponent along, and it was not to be wondered that there should be tired men in the tanks. Gaudaur was fourth man to make the turn, his followers being, in succession, Lee, Ten Eyck, Delano, Plaisted, and Boyd, the last-named seemingly distressed, and as he fouled his buoy in turning, whereby he lost valuable time and distance, he evidently now regarded his case as hopeless, and did not afterwards make an effort to win anything, although continuing on down the river. Dempsey did not go to the stake at all, having had enough of it before reaching that point.

The pull back taxed the strength and skill of the oarsmen to the utmost, as soon after rounding the buoys the wind increased greatly in force, breaking the water up into good-sized hillocks, surmounted with white-caps, and it was a difficult matter to keep one's shell from swamping, while all were obliged to carry water home with them. It was astonishing to see the way in which Ross, who had earned the title of champion smooth-water man, made his shell travel through the young sea; but then he was the only man who had taken the precaution to fit his boat with a wind-sail, which, with that wind to contend against, was a really necessary article, and would have materially helped all who tried it. When about two and one quarter miles had: been rowed Hanlan was again seen to quit rowing, and an inquiry from those on the press-boat elicited a reply by signal, he placing his hand to his side to indicate that the trouble was there. He did not persevere, merely paddling down to the boathouse, arriving long after the winner had been made known. Ten Eyck succeeded in wresting the third prize from Gaudaur. Time: Ross, 29m. 54s.; Riley, 30m. 30½s.; Ten Eyck, 30m. 58s. A roar of applause greeted Ross at the finish, and then the people hurried back to the city, surprised but not displeased at the result of the race.

Hanlan's trouble was stated to be a severe pain in the side, which first attacked him in Washington, and on account of which he for some time wore a plaster over the affected part, this bringing him the desired relief, when he dispensed with the plaster. The reason given for Boyd's failure to do better is that he was not in as good condition as such a hard race required. The prizes were presented at the Coliseum, a mammoth pavilion at Rocky Point. After the presentation a number of invited guests were entertained by the E. R. A. at the hotel at the Point.

TRICKETT AT NEWCASTLE: NOVEMBER 15, 1880

In the meantime, Hanlan had, after numerous endeavors, been matched to row Edward A. Trickett, of Sydney, Australia, who claimed to hold the title of Champion Oarsman of the World. A match was made for the rival oarsman to row over the Tyne Championship Course for £400, Championship, and the Sportsman Challenge Champion Cup that Hanlan had won from Elliott. All the preliminaries for the match were quickly and satisfactorily arranged. Trickett arrived in England in company with his Australian backers and Laycock, a noted oarsman. He went directly into training, and displayed great form. Hanlan arrived on the Thames soon after, but rowed his trials well within himself, so that the Australian sporting men were confident that Trickett would defeat Hanlan. The race was rowed over the Thames Championship Course on November 15th, 1880, a day long to be remembered in the history of international aquatic contests. ....

Hanlan used his white cedar boat built by George Wharin, of Toronto, and rowed in his well-known suit of blue. Trickett used a boat built at Newcastle, and rowed stripped to the waist. On account of the crookedness of the course, it is customary in England to allow to each sculler a pilot, who sits in the bow of an eight-oared cutter, follows closely behind the contestants, and steers his man by shout and gesture.

The weather was unpleasant. During the early morning an unusually cold, thick, clammy fog enveloped London, and during the forenoon this mass of mist seemed to melt into a steady, drizzling rain. About noon the fog became so thin that the assembled crowds could see across the river, and when the race was started, at 12:14 P.M., the weather was cool and damp, but without actual rain, the tide almost full and flooding slowly, a very light wind from northwest, and water as smooth as could be wished.

The race, if race it can be called, hardly merits description, and was a farce of the broadest sort. From numerous independent despatches we arrange the following account:

The start was made from boats moored 25 yards apart, opposite the Star and Garter Hotel. Trickett won the toss, and choosed the Middlesex, or right hand side, but there was little choice in the actual condition of wind and tide, Hanlan seemed in perfect condition, cheerful, confident, and even playful. Trickett appeared to be a trifle overtrained, and looked sallow, careworn, and anxious. Each man, however, expressed himself as in good health, well-trained, satisfactorily equipped, ready to row the race without excuses, and to acknowledge the winner as the best man. Trickett's backers also were satisfied with his condition, and invested their money freely, even after the men were in their boats. It is, therefore, probable that Trickett's appearance was due to his personal habits and physical characteristics, and that his anxious, careworn looks were usual to him, and not significant of poor condition.

At the moment when the struggle commenced there was an easily observable contrast in the demeanor of the men. Trickett had evidently braced himself up. Some moments before he dipped his sculls into the water for his initial stroke his legs were firmly set, and there was a brave look of determination about him. His face was careworn, as he had appeared when preparing for the contest; the lines in his countenance were now much more prominent, and he seemed positively haggard. Hanlan, on the contrary, maintained a cheerful, almost rollicking demeanor. The air of bravado with which he had gambolied in the stake boat had not deserted him, and he did not look as though embarking on a race concerning which so many interests were at issue. At the very moment when he got underway he was apparently engaged in criticising his rival, and it was not until the contending boats were well on the move that he turned his eyes toward the stern of his skiff and devoted the whole of his energies to the business in hand. During the first minute Hanlan rowed 35 strokes, Trickett 40, and it was evident, thus early, that the Canadian had the race at his mercy. He was sculling easily, and plainly within himself, while Trickett labored heavily, and was clearly exerting himself to the utmost limit of his powers. At the mile post the time was not taken, as the press boat was too far behind. Hanlan was about a couple of lengths to the good, and this advantage he did not seem to care to increase. At the Crab Tree (time 6m. 4s.) about the same distance separated the boats, and immediately afterward Trickett improved visibly. He not only held his own, but had the best of the pace up to the Soap Works, at which point (time 7m. 46s.) he was about a length and a half in the rear, Hanlan nodded affably to the applauding multitude, and devoted so much attention to them that he steered right out of his course, veering over for the northern shore. But a single vigorous stroke with his left put the boat straight again, and he now demonstrated that he considered he had a comparatively easy task before him, for he sculled in a literally lazy style. However, he braced up again as Suspension Bridge, with throngs of excited onlookers, was neared, and treated the assemblage to an exhibition of his marvelous skill, passing beneath the structure with a couple of lengths in hand. His time to this point was 9m. 31s., and Trickett's, 9m. 34s.

He kept on at his smart pace until off Biffen's Boat-house, where he treated the onlookers to a dose of those remarkable maneuvers which created such in tense astonishment among the multitudes who saw him contend with Hawdon on the Tyne. Ceasing to row for a moment, he leaned back in his boat and indulged in a leisurely survey of the scenery, and when he once more got to work it was in a half-hearted way, as though he would prefer to linger, did not circumstances compel his progressing. Before he had gone thirty yards, however, he stopped again, and having thoroughly got his hand in at this game he continually repeated it.

Trickett was another sorrowful spectacle from the start. He had kept his eyes on his mentor, Kelly, and no one accused him of neglecting his task for a single instant, but there was a painful lack of power about his manipulation of the sculls, and it was evident before Hammersmith was reached that the exertion he had made had told upon him very seriously. His face had assumed a leaden hue, and it grew well-nigh livid as he approached the Doves. With fast decreasing energy he kept on, and the wild expression of his countenance marvellously contrasted with the demeanor of his opponent.

About the Oil Mills a large flotilla of small craft encumbered the river, but they kept fairly out of the way,

though Hanlan seemed to entertain suspicions that he
might come into collision with one of them, as he
constantly looked around. Having apparently satisfied
himself that all was right he dashed in half a dozen
vigorous strokes and was quickly four lengths ahead. He
now attempted a piece of harlequinade, the like which was
never before witnessed in a race. Dropping his sculls
clumsily into the water, he fell right forward upon his face
and lay there for a second or two. So long did he remain in
a recumbent position that a kind of groan came from the
spectators, who imagined something terrible had befallen
him, but before they could find their voices to shout and
inquire what was the matter he had sprung up, suddenly
resumed the sculls, and was at work again, laughing
merrily. A roar of laughter greeted this feat, and it was
some minutes before the intense excitement occasioned by
it had abated.

Trickett had meanwhile approached within two lengths,
but he had no power left to draw nearer, and Hanlan,
apparently as fresh as the moment he started, went away
again with consummate ease. He had a spell of rowing
with alternate sculls, stopped repeatedly, looked anywhere
but at his pilot, dawdled in every conceivable style, and
generally was as full of antics as a clown. His time to
Chiswick Church was 15m. 34s. Trickett was three lengths
behind. A little further on Elliott was observed ahead,
pulling in the direction of Barnes. Hanlan pulled toward
him and the pair went on in company, maintaining an
animated conversation.

All along the Duke of Devonshire's meadows this farce
was kept up. Hanlan and Elliott rowing leisurely side by
side, talking, and Trickett, with blanched face and labored
breathing, toiling in the rear. As the Bulls Head, at Barnes,
was neared, Hanlan bore away from the Middlesex shore
once more. Some of the inspired ones in the press boat
now burst into prophesy. They observed that Hanlan had
threatened to beat Trickett out of sight, and they imagined

he was about to commence that effort. Really there seemed some ground for the supposition, for the Canadian had squared his shoulders, and was skimming along at a rapid pace.

This newly developed energy was evanescent. In a second or two he dropped his sculls, dipped his right hand in the river, and scooped up the water, nodding genially in the direction of the approaching steamers. He pretended to drink, then smoothed his hair, passed his palm across his brow, and once more resumed work in a languid fashion. By this time Elliott was once more alongside, and the political or social discussion was resumed.

In the vicinity of Hanlan's training quarters, the Bull's Head, an immense concourse had assembled, and they applauded lustily as he was seen with a commanding lead, and progressing at his ease. He ceased to work, and drawing forth a white handkerchief, waved it gracefully in the direction of his admirers, while peals of laughter and rounds of cheers greeted him time after time. He passed beneath Barnes Bridge in 21m. 40s. from the start. Trickett, utterly jaded and worn out, passed under 9 seconds later. Thenceforth the pair plodded on steadily, Hanlan gazing about him with supreme indifference. A cannon shot announced the arrival of Hanlan at the winning post in 26m. 12s. Trickett's time was 26m. 19s. Trickett stopped exactly opposite the flag-staff, and apparently was not sorry that the journey was over. Mr. Moore, the distance judge, gave the verdict that the race was won by three lengths.

We publish this long and rambling description of the match because in no other way could we so clearly show the absolute hollowness of the race and the marked superiority of Hanlan to Trickett. The Australian was a man who had been tried thoroughly and successfully and was heavily backed by cool-headed experts, yet Hanlan made child's play of the race, and beat him with the same ridiculous ease that marked his triumphs over Courtney, Riley, Hawdon, and Elliott.

The affair was a procession, not a race, and the Canadian to speak after the manner of man-made a holy show of his Australian opponent. The walk over, for such it was, offers no point of special interest, and the match is only noteworthy as a remarkable example of mistaken judgment by men who are, or should be, experts.

For a month before the race Hanlan was hard at work on the same course with Trickett, and the Australian party had every opportunity to watch his daily practice, to see him row his trial spins, to time him over measured fractional portions of the course, But nothing that they thus saw and heard could shake their blind confidence in the Australian giant. They backed him freely and persistently, from the day of their arrival to the day of the race, and all sensational stories about Trickett's ill health, poor condition and over-training are swept away by the simple fact that his backers were full of confidence and betting their money freely up to the very moment of starting.

On this side of the Atlantic they followed similar tactics. They took all offered bets, deposited round sums of Tricket money in all the prominent sporting resorts, actually bet New York City to a stand-still, and the market, an hour before the race, could have been correctly quoted:

"—offering united sums on Trickett, with no takers."

And yet in the race, Trickett never had the ghost of a chance, and Hanlan actually made sport of him, and played monkey capers all over the river in a race which decided more money than any ever rowed in the world.

Not only were the Australians deceived, but many of England's aquatic experts backed Trickett freely; and no one of them all, after seeing the men at their work, doubted that the race would be close and severe. It is almost incomprehensible that so many intelligent men could have been so strangely wrong, and it would seem that aquatic knowledge and experience are practically useless in judging the abilities of individual scullers.

Perhaps in the history of boating there was never so much excitement over a race or such a vast amount of money wagered as on the great contest between Hanlan and Trickett. Trickett's backers were the Thompson brothers, well-known bookmakers, Sydney, New South Wales. One of them, Barney, soft Sydney April 22nd, duly authorized to make a Hanlan-Trickett match in America. He arrived in New York in early June, and attended the Providence regatta. After seeing Ross, Hanlan, Boyd, and all the other scullers at practice and in the actual race, he felt assured that his man could easily row away from the whole fleet. Alas! The losses of the Thompsons were enormous.

Regarding the Champions contest with Trickett, the London *Sporting Life* published the following remarks:

> Of the race itself, there is not much to say. Trickett could not go fast enough to give Hanlan serious trouble, and after he had played with his man for a few hundred yards the Canadian merely kept his opponent at full tension till he had rowed himself out. The result of Trickett's exertions shows the value of the term a 'stayer.' Trickett was to have rowed the last mile faster than the first, and so very likely he would had he been allowed to make his own pace, As it was, he was obliged to bustle himself from the outset, and tired to a standstill before Hammersmith Bridge was reached. He persevered gamely enough, but all the fire and strength were gone, all his faults became exaggerated. Hanlan's sculling was worth travelling a hundred miles to see and was just as good as the others was weak. Trickett, with all his long inboard, made small use of his natural advantages of reach, and as he tired, did nearly all his work with his arms alone, taking a very short stroke. Some excuse may be made for him, as he was overtrained if not ill; but, fit and well, he is not of the same class as the Canadian. Hanlan's style has already been described, and as he never allowed himself to be in any way flurried he showed to great advantage. His victory was very popular, as he was the public favorite of the two. Trickett has

managed to make himself anything but liked at Putney a curious thing, as Mr. Thompson and Laycock have everyone's good word; the other has not made friends where he might.

Hanlan, perhaps thoughtlessly, has lowered himself in the estimation of many well-thinking people. The clowning business in which he indulged when he had Trickett beaten was very foolish. It is quite possible that he was only giving vent to his satisfaction at finding he had such a good thing on, but consideration for the feelings of his plucky opponent ought to have kept him from showing anything but respect for him, beaten as he was. Another way of looking at this tricky performance is suggested by the possibility of his having lost the race through it. Suppose that when he invited accident he had brought about some mishap, how much of his own and his backers money would have been sacrificed for the sake of senseless larking? Worse than all, he might someday find he had cried *Wolf!* too often, and not got assistance when he had really met with an accident. In carrying thousands of pounds entrusted to his skill he had a heavy responsibility, and, moreover, after the show he made of Trickett, may be a long while before he gets another chance of so easily earning a fortune. Besides, there should be a certain amount of dignity attaching to the possession of the title of *Champion*, and tricks certainly do not add to the value of his position. The main thing is, though, that while exposing himself and his backers to unnecessary risk, his behavior can be construed as ungenerous to Trickett. As a rule, watermen's desire of achieving fame outlives their powers of execution, and no best performer of his day has, in our time, at any rate, learned the decadence of his powers before defeat has rudely forced the unpleasant fact upon him. From this, if from no nigher feeling, consideration for the beaten cannot be too strongly insisted on. Apart from the unpleasant episode just dealt with, Hanlan's exhibition was splendid, and his superiority markedly established. For Trickett, it is hard lines to have come so far to experience such a decisive reverse, and he and his party are heavy losers. It is poor consolation for the second to know that in a match someone must lose; let us hope that Trickett's next engagement after he has recovered his health may help to make amends for his recent defeat. If the contest be taken a test of the merits of the Australian method of sculling, the very much cross handed business may be considered as done with.

After Elias C. Laycock, of Sydney, Australia, won the first prize in the International Thames Regatta, his admirers authorized him to challenge Hanlan to row for £200 a side. Hanlan refused to row unless he was allowed six weeks to train, he having gained over ten pounds since he ran away from Trickett, on November 15, 1880, besides, he had sold his racing shells. Hanlan finally decided to meet Laycock and row for £500 and the championship of England, and the race was fixed for January 17th, 1881. Hanlan would have rowed for the Championship of the World, but he desired to row any man in the world for that title on Toronto Bay during 1881. About the time Hanlan and Laycock were arranging the preliminaries for the race, the Toronto *Globe* published the following:

It has always been very hard for the *Spirit of the Times* to acknowledge Hanlan's supremacy as a sculler, but now that he has literally made a show of every American oarsman who lays claim to any degree of prominence, any but the most pronounced of braggarts would be quite ready to own up and accept the inevitable; but that is just the hardest task that can be set for the average through and through Yankee to accomplish, and if there's a man and a journal that are typical Yankees in this respect the man is Charles E. Courtney, and the journal is the *Spirit of the Times*. Before the race at Lachine, Courtney was sure he could beat Hanlan, and a few days later, after Hanlan had good-naturedly conceded him a close finish there, the big duffer was again boasting that he could beat the Canadian. They met at Chautauqua Lake, and before Courtney would go out upon the water he wanted a promise from Hanlan in writing that he (Courtney) would be allowed to win, and when he found that Hanlan meant to pull the race on his merits he sawed his boats to sneak out of the contest. At last they met at Washington, and

Hanlan made a sorry exhibition of the Union Springs man, just as he had promised to do if ever he caught him on the water again. And yet after all this the *Spirit of the Times* has the assurance to say: if a certain American sculler had Laycock's heart inside his vest, the Champion of the World would have lived in New York since 1876. What in the name of common sense has Courtney ever done to warrant such an impudent assertion? Admitting that Hanlan frightened the heart out of him at Lachine, and that thirty or forty thousand dollars from Toronto frightened the hearts out of the so-called sporting men who followed him, so that before the race came off it was hard to get money on Hanlan at any odds, that is no reason why Courtney should tremble at the mention of Trickett's name; and yet if Trickett ever comes to this part of the world to row a race with Courtney the Australians will have to put their money on at three to one. If, as the *Spirit of the Times* still persists or impudently insinuating, Courtney can row five miles in less time than Hanlan can, he surely need not be afraid to row against a man with whom Hanlan literally played. The big Yankee would not require the heart of a British colonist under his vest to win such an easy race as that would be; and yet if Courtney and his twin brother, who edits the aquatic portion of the *Spirit of the Times*, could only muster sufficient courage to make such a match and win if they could take more money out of the Australians than would cover the combined losses of all American citizens who have from time to time taken the short end of it against Hanlan. They could in their own classical vernacular win barrels of money. But of course, they won't do it. They might possibly bring in some sort of a race for a purse, but when it came to risking any money they wouldn't put in a cent.

The same article, a large portion of which was forwarded to us by telegraph and published some days since, closes with the following allusion to Hanlan:

But the general public will hardly fall to believe that he avoided the regatta because Ross was a dangerous customer, and now runs away from Laycock be owe in a contest with him, there would be blows to receive as well as blows to give.

If Hanlan was afraid of Ross, why did he row him down on Toronto Bay, on the Kennebeccasis, and on Kempenfeldt Bay? If he was afraid of Laycock why did he engage in a match with Trickett, who at the time was supposed to be Laycock's superior. If he is anxious to run away from Laycock, why does he want to raise the stake from £200 to £1,000. If he feared a beating one would imagine that he would like to have it cost himself and his friends as little as possible. The truth of the matter is simply this : Hanlan cannot make his record more illustrious by defeating any sculler now before the public, and he would be very foolish to engage in another contest the winnings of which would be eaten up between loss of time and expenses. He has only acted in a common sense manner in insisting that his next race, if it be rowed away from home, shall be for a sum more than sufficient to cover loss of time and expenses. If the Australians think Laycock can beat him they will put up the money fast enough; and if they do not, they have no business to ask him to remain over merely to lead another procession from Putney to Mortlake.

❧ 5 ❧

1880: PROVIDENCE, RI

International Scullers
Amateur and Professional Races at Providence
Wallace Ross' Star in the Ascendant
His Triumph Over the Champion of two Continents
The St. John Sculler wins as he pleases
Twenty Lengths Ahead of Riley, the Second Man
Hanlan Becomes Ill and Gives Up

PROVIDENCE, R.I., June 17th, 1880.*

Probably the city of Providence never saw as many people within its limits as gathered on the banks of the Seekonk to-day. The number is variously estimated from 40,000 to 100,000. They came by rail, street car, sailboat, barges, steamers and every conceivable mode of conveyance. It was a peaceable crowd, all intent on seeing the grand race, but the proportion that had any definite idea of who started to row crowded with craft of all descriptions, whose occupants thought the best position for viewing the race was between the grandstands, of which there were a dozen or more, along the course. The press facilities were poor, also for the same reason inefficient or rather, utter want of police on the course.

---

* *The Daily Telegraph*, St. John, N.B. Friday, June 18, 1880.

THE PROFESSIONAL RACE: ROSS AN EARLY WINNER

Another long wait occurred with the professionals in line before they started which they did at 5. 29. 42 p.m.

The following men appeared on the course and took up positions as drawn:

No. Name Residence

1- Wallace Ross St. John, N.B.
2- Geo, W. Lec Newark, N.J.
3- Jas. H Riley Saratoga Springs
4- Horatio K.N. Delano Chelsea, Mass
5- Jas. A. Ten Eyck Peeksill, N.Y.
6- Fred A. Plaisted Boston
7- Jacob Gaudier Toronto
8- Jas. H. Dempsey Geneva, N.Y.
9- Robt. W. Boyd Middlesboro, Eng.
10- Edward Hanlan Toronto

Geo. Hosmer, of Boston, Weidberger of Wheeling, West Virginia, and Frenchy Johnson did not row and No.8 place drawn by Hosmer gave an advantage to those who followed.

At the start Plaisted fairly jumped his shell to the front, and Ross was close at his heels, while over on the cast Providence side Hanlan and Boyd were seen almost together. The two latter kept at it for about 60 strokes when the champion shot away ahead of the Britisher, and began to creep up to Plaisted, who was the leader, and right nobly was he cutting out the pace. Ross was close behind him, however, and at the quarter was on even terms. The Hanlan, who had left Boyd, began to tell with his powerful regular strokes, and slowly to creep up to Ross. So tremendous was his speed that at the half mile he had about half a length lead over the field. A prettier sight has seldom been witnessed than was presented by those four men who were rowing nearly abreast, straining every nerve for the mastery. Hanlan, Ross, Plaisted, and Riley, who had come up rapidly on

the finish of the first mile away, went from half a mile to mile and a half.

Hanlan Stops Rowing

The champion, to the surprise of those who could see the course, stopped rowing, and Ross swept grandly ahead, with Plaisted and Riley neck and neck just behind. While the leaders were struggling so gallantly Lee, Ten Eyck and Gaudier were having a close contest among themselves, while Dempsey, Delano and Boyd were in another triangular contest and brought up the rear of the procession. Hanlan, when he stopped rowing, put his hand to his side as if in pain for a moment.

Then he pulled his sculls with determination and rowed with a will, holding second place to the turn, which he made immediately after Ross. From then to the finish he slacked up and rowed home leisurely.

Ross Comes In The Winner

Ross, seeing that Hanlan was disabled also turned buoy No. 2, and squared away homeward at a magnificent pace, leading the field by at least 20 lengths to the finish, crossing the line in 28min. 54 sec., an easy winner, amid the cheers of thousands of spectators and salvos from the yachts round about.

Plaisted and Riley, after a struggle and great liability of fouling, turned the stake together. As soon as they were fairly on their way home Riley, by extra exertions, managed to catch Plaisted, and was away a dozen lengths, ahead.

Riley Passes Hanlan

At the two-mile stake, he passed Hanlan and securely settled down to second place which he gained without much further effort, passing the stake boat in 30 min. 50 seconds, five or six lengths ahead of Gaudier, who finished a length ahead of Plaisted. The boat of the latter was half full of water. Craft on craft on the river now crowded in at the general turn over the finish, thus shutting out the others and the great race was over.

The only accident to mar the day's pleasure was the fall of about 150 feet of one of the grandstands, by which Mrs. Mary Wallace, of Boston, was severely and several people injured. A number of others became panic-stricken and jumped overboard, but escaped with a wetting.

Various rumors are abroad to-night relative to Hanlan's giving out, but Referee Curtis says he was out of condition and lost the race through illness caused by not being acclimated.

Over Eleven Professionals at the Oar

The professional event — the great trial of skill that the vast multitude came to see — was next in order. While the amateur race was progressing the professionals, except Boyd, were gathered on the veranda in rear of Brown's University boat house engaged in pleasant conversation, all seemingly in the best of condition and spirits.

Called Out

About 5:10 the gun for them to get ready was fired and they soon started for the referee's boat. Hanlan had just started and quickened a little when the signal was made and he rowed towards the grandstand. He was the cynosure of many eyes ashore and afloat while loud applause greeted him during his pull to the starting point. Lee, Gaudier, Ten Eyck, Riley, Delano, Ross, Plaisted and Dempsey followed in the order named while Boyd soon arrived from his quarters at Ten Mile River.

Kennedy and Hosmer did not out in an appearance.

Hanlan and Ross

Hanlan looked the picture of good health; his skin clear and his eyes bright and sparkling. All the others were in good condition, Ross particularly so, the latter winning many favorable comments on his style, which has vastly improved.

The course could not have been better. It ran nearly due north and south, the start and finish being nearly opposite a high cliff called Walker's Point. At the southern end the course is as straight as an arrow and a splendid breadth of water is allowed for turns.

The amateurs turned a short distance past Back-Jin Island, and the professional turn was brought just opposite Ingrahamville, in 2,000 feet of water. Ample room was thus afforded for turning the stakes for each contestant, fouling being rendered impossible.

A splendid start was effected at 5.27 p.m. Hanlan and Ross at once struck out ahead of the others Ross slightly in advance. Boyd passed him, and Riley close behind. At the end of the first half mile Hanlan led with Boyd second, Riley third and Ross a bad fourth, Plaisted fifth and the rest behind. This order maintained at the first-mile stake, but half a mile further on in the contest Plaisted crept to second with the remained in a solid bunch and soon pressed Hanlan hard; at the turn Plaisted amid cheers of those assembled at that point, passed the champion and maintained it for the next half mile; When the fact was noted on bulletin boards at the telephone exchange great excitement, prevailed and Plaisted stock began to rise in the pool market. The dash of lightening in the sculler did not last, however, and he slowly dropped behind, Hanlan, Boyd and Riley passing him in succession with Ross dangerously near. This was the position at the end of the three miles, and Ross then began to send his boat along with renewed and terrific force, passing Plaisted, Riley, then Boyd, finally Hanlan. This feat of the New Brunswick champion was greeted with cheers from the large multitude, who shouted themselves hoarse. Hanlan's friends shouted words of encouragement, but they met with no response, and he was shortly passed Plaisted, Riley and Boyd. The order at the three-and-a-half stake was: Ross, Riley, Ten Eyck and Boyd and from that to the close Ross had everything his own way, coming down the last half mile in fine style, having won the prize of $3000.

Riley finished second and Ten Eyck third. Hanlan came in fifth, apparently disabled, and is reported sick to-night. Whether this is so or not cannot be ascertained, but it is certain that when he started he was looking remarkably well. Boyd finished well in fifth place, while the others were far in the rear.

Thousands of visitors left for home by special trains to-night, but still a large number remain, and many will have to go without a bed.

The presentation of prizes took place at the Coliseum, Rocky Point, steamers conveying crowds from the city. Ross was received with wild applause and was presented with the first prize by Governor Littlefield, of Rhode Island. He made a modest reply. The other oarsmen were well received. Holmes, the amateur winner, had an enthusiastic reception and was the recipient of the elegant trophy. The proceedings came to a close about ten o'clock.

A Report That Hanlan Will Challenge Ross

It is reported that Hanlan at once will challenge Ross to row on the Seekonk again.

The result of the race, for the most part, was unexpected, it being generally considered that Hanlan was a sure winner. Ross' chances for second place was considered good but few thought that he would be winner.

In the pool selling, just before the race, Hanlan was the favorite by 100 to 40. The field was about one and a half to one over either Ross, Riley or Boyd, barring Hanlan.

•••

Opinion of the Toronto "Globe." Toronto, June 17th

The *Globe* will editorially express surprise at the result of the Providence regatta, that Hanlan should have been beaten by Ross and Plaisted, whom he formerly distanced so far and who have so often been beaten by others. Hanlan's plea of illness will, however, be for the present accepted as *bon a fide*.

Sheriff Harding's Opinion of the Victory of Ross

A representative of the Telegraph called on Sheriff Harding, last night at his residence, Waterloo street, and had a pleasant chat with the Sheriff about Ross, his abilities and his idea as to how the St. John sculler came to win this regatta race. The Sheriff remarked, when the object of the mission was made known, that he, being here in St. John, could not be expected to know much about the race; how it was rowed, etc., and the telegrams, he sagely remarked, did not lend assistance of material value upon which to gauge a reason for the result-Ross won. The telegrams say, said the Sheriff, Ross won, Plaisted second, Boyd third, Hanlan not placed. Now, continued he, if no accident happened Hanlan has lost by rowing three races within a month, was pressed by the field and Ross, keeping within himself till near the finish, with a burst rowed all competitors down. Hanlan has heretofore (except at Barrie) rowed all of his opponents down within a mile, then stopped, taken a full breath and naturally, being a man of good lungs, was ready to take a fresh dash. And this is in my opinion where Hanlan's great success lies. He is able to row his opponent down within a mile of the goal and then take a good full breath and pull with renewed vigor. But if a man can be got who can row Hanlan the course over and give him no chance to renew his wind, then you have the man who can beat him. But Hanlan has the natural abilities for his adopted profession, and a man of that kind in any line is hard to excel. But this time — this race at Providence — he has probably been pressed, his previous work has told on him and, having no time to catch his wind, has burst.

Reporter: Well, what about Ross, can he beat Hanlan?

The Sheriff: He cannot, and never could and never will beat Hanlan. Though I have always looked upon Ross as the second best oarsman in America, yet he cannot beat Hanlan.

Reporter: When did you first see Hanlan?

Sheriff: The first time I saw Hanlan was on the Schuylkill, and then I made up my mind that he was the best man that had appeared yet. There are no whims nor notions about him, he is a thoroughly practical man, a man as I have said before, naturally adapted as a professional oarsman. When he rowed in England against Elliott you will remember he took a trip to Scotland under the guise of seeing the elephant, but his trip was a part of his training. He went away and let nature recuperate herself. He is a man possessed of strong powerful lungs, as anybody can infer for himself, but he is only human and can be over-worked. Now you know, as well as I do, that this Providence race is the third within a month. This exertion would tell on any human being. But you know, or it is generally known that there is money at the back of all these races.

Reporter: Gambling?

Sheriff: Yes, gambling it is. But do not understand me that I insinuate that Hanlan's backers would sell a race. They will not do that, (said the Sheriff) seriously. But they will give a race and there is a vast difference between selling a race and giving a race.

Reporter: As Chief Justice Allen says, there is a vast difference between murdering a man and murdering a ship?

Sheriff: Yes, I should think there was. But, (continued the Sheriff) Hanlan is soon to row Trickett. This regatta is a good medium by which to show to the world that he can be beaten as well as be victorious. If he should go to England with a record showing that he was born to conquer, all betting would be one-sided, except that the few Australians who might come over with Trickett, would back their man.

Reporter: Hanlan's backers would not sell a race then you think?

Sheriff: No they would not. I am positive of that. They could have no object in selling a race; they would lose more than they would gain in the end. Indeed they have no need to entertain any such thoughts.

Reporter: Is there not some intention of matching Ross against Hanlan?

Sheriff: There is a feeling that way perhaps, but it is a foolish idea. St. John men had better keep their money in their pockets, for there is not a doubt, as I already stated, but that Hanlan can beat Ross.

In closing the interview with the Sheriff, he submitted the following query: Is it becoming a custom for flyers to take a step down in the scale of success that they may be sensational?

THE ILLUSTRATED LONDON NEWS

REGISTERED AT THE GENERAL POST-OFFICE FOR TRANSMISSION ABROAD.

No. 2164.—VOL. LXXVII.　　　SATURDAY, NOVEMBER 20, 1880.　　　WITH TWO SUPPLEMENTS　SIXPENCE By Post, 6½d.

CHAMPIONSHIP SCULLING-MATCH

*Except on the occasion of an Inter-University Boat-race, or of the famous contests between Oxford and Harvard Universities, and the London and Atalanta Rowing Clubs, we never saw so many people between Putney and Mortlake as were assembled there on Monday morning.

The weather was singularly uninviting, as it was decidedly raw and cold, and a drizzling rain fell at intervals; but the towing-path was well patronised for the whole distance, whilst at Hammersmith, Barnes, and one or two other favourite places, the crowds were very dense.

Popular feeling seemed to have completely changed again, and was all in favour of Hanlan, though two days before slight odds were laid on Trickett. The previous achievements of the two men are so well known that we need only touch upon them slightly.

Edward Hanlan, of Toronto, is twenty-five years of age, stands just under 5 ft. 9 in., and weights 10 st. 12 lb. After a career of almost unbroken success in America, he came to England last year, and defeated Elliott and Hawdon in much style that it appeared hopeless for him to get any more matches in this country. He has carried off other prizes in America since then, but cut up very badly in the Hop Bitters Regatta (1879), his explanation being that he was taken ill during the race.

Edward Trickett, of Sydney, New South Wales, is four years

---

*　*London Illustrated News,* November 20, 1880, p.506.

older than his late opponent, is not less than 6 ft. 3 and a half in. in height, but, being of spare frame, only weighs 12 st. 5 lb. in strict training. He has beaten all the best men in his own country, and, in 1876, he came to England, and made a sad example of Joseph Sadler, who, though champion of England at the time, had undoubtedly seen his best day.

Both men have been located on the banks of the Thames— Trickett at Putney and his rival at Barnes—for some weeks past, and their practice has been watched with very great interest.

The race was fixed for twelve o'clock, but it was past that time before the competitors put off from the shore. Harry Kelley piloted the Australian, and Bright performed the same office for Hanlan, who looked wonderfully well and full of spirits and confidence, while his opponent, whose face is naturally rather haggard and careworn, seemed very anxious.

There was little or no tide, but the river was perfectly smooth, and Trickett gained scarcely any advantage from winning the toss and selecting the Middlesex station. There is little to say relative to the race itself, as it was really all over before they reached Hammersmith Bridge. Trickett began with a faster stroke than Hanlan, but he was sliding very short, and seemed to trust mainly to his immense strength to drive his boat along.

The Canadian, whose style is simply perfect, and has never been approached by that of any other sculler, at once took a slight lead, and appeared to wait in front until nearing Hammersmith Bridge, when he began to open out a gap between himself and Trickett, and the latter being in evident trouble, though persevering as gamely as possible, the contest was virtually at an end.

Hanlan was not long in finding out the state of affairs, and consequently could not resist from indulging in a series of wild antics, similar to those he went through on his previous visit here, during his matches with Elliott and Hawdon; and, had he lost the race in consequence, he would have had but a few sympathisers.

Just below the Doves, he put in "half-a-dozen" to show the spectators how much he had in hand, and then, clumsily dropping his sculls into the water, threw himself flat on his back in the

bottom of the boat, and lay there for a second or two, the act occasioning great excitement amongst the large number of spectators who witness it, for they naturally imagined that something terrible had befallen him; however, he was soon up and at work again, laughing heartily.

The Canadian made at least half a dozen further stoppages before Barnes Bridge was reached, on each occasion going through a little performance, such as washing his face, kissing his hand, and cheerfully waving his handkerchief to different friends on the bank, and he eventually won at his leisure by three lengths, which he could have made a quarter of a mile had he so chosen, the time being 26 min. 12 sec.

It is a pity the winner indulged in the clowning business to the extent he did, for though possibly he was only giving vent to his satisfaction at finding himself master of the situation, still consideration for the feelings of his plucky opponent ought to have kept him from showing anything but respect for a beaten man. Apart from this, Hanlan's exhibition was splendid, and his superiority established beyond doubt. It is poor consolation for the second to know that in a match someone must lose, but let us hope that Trickett's next engagement may help to make amends for his recent defeat.

W.B. Woodgate, *Boating*, 1889.*

Hanlan first attracted notice at the Philadelphia regatta of 1876. Mr. R. H. Labat, of the Dublin University, London, and Thames Rowing Clubs, took part in that regatta, and entered into conversation with Hanlan. He, as one of the L.R.C. men, lent Hanlan a pair of sculls for the occasion, and with them Hanlan won the Open Professional Sculling Prize. He beat among others one Luke, who had beaten Higgins in a trial heat. Higgins was at the moment suffering from exertions in a four-oared race earlier in the day, so that his defeat did not occasion much surprise; but

* W.B. Woodgate, *Boating*, 2nd Ed. (London: Longmans, Green & Co., 1889), 226-231.

Mr. Labat on his return to England told the writer of this chapter
that in his opinion Hanlan was far and away the best sculler he
had ever seen, and that even if Higgins had been fresh and fit,
Hanlan would have been too good for him. At that date Hanlan
had not made his great reputation, but the soundness of Mr.
Labat's estimate of his powers was fully verified subsequently.

In 1879 Hanlan, having beaten the best American scullers,
came to England to row for the *Sportsman* Challenge Cup. He
commenced his career in England by beating a second-rate
northern sculler, in a sort of trial match; but this was only a feeler
before trying conclusions with Elliott. The two met on the Tyne
on June 16, and Elliott was simply 'never in it.' Hanlan led him,
played with him, and beat him as he liked.

It did not require any very deep knowledge of oarsmanship to
enable a spectator to observe the vast difference which existed
between his style and that of such men as Boyd or Elliott. Hanlan
used his slide concurrently with swing, carrying his body well
back, with straight arms long past the perpendicular, before he
attempted to row the stroke in by bending the arms. His
superiority was manifest, and yet our British (professional) scullers
seemed wedded to this vicious trick of premature slide and no
swing, and doggedly declined to recognise the maxim:

> *Fas est et ab hoste doceri.* (Ovid)
> One must also be taught by enemies.

At that rate, the two best British scullers were, in the writer's
opinion, two amateurs—viz., Mr. Frank Playford, holder of the
Wingfield Sculls, and Mr. T. C. Edwardes-Moss, twice winner of
the Diamonds at Henley. Either of these gentlemen could have
made a terrible example of the best British professionals, could
amateur etiquette have admitted a match between the two classes.
The only time that these gentlemen met, Mr. Playford proved the
winner, over the Wingfield course. A sort of line as to relative
merit between amateur and professional talent is gained by
recalling Mr. Edwardes-Moss's victory for the Diamond Sculls in
1878. In that year he met an American, Lee, then self-styled an

amateur, but who now openly practises as a professional, and who is quite in the first flight of that class in America. He could probably beat any English professional of today, or at least make a close fight with our best man. When the two met at Henley Mr. Edwardes-Moss was by no means in trim to uphold the honour of British sculling. He had gone through three commemoration balls at Oxford about ten days before the regatta. He had only an old sculling boat, somewhat screwed and limp. He had lent her freely to Eton and Windsor friends during the preceding summer, not anticipating that he would need her to race in again; but when the regatta drew nigh he could find no boat to suit him, and had to make shift with the old boat. In the race he had to give Lee the inside, or Berks station; and all who have known Henley Regatta are well aware of the advantage of that side; it gives dead water for some hundreds of yards below Poplar Point, and still further gains on rounding the point. Three lengths would fairly represent the minimum of the handicap between the two stations on a smooth day, such as that of the race. The two scullers raced round the point, Lee leading slightly; but the Oxonian caught him and just headed him on the post. Lee stopped one stroke too soon, whether from exhaustion or error is uncertain, but the performance plainly stamped the English amateur as his superior, half-trained and badly boated as he was. Over a champion course, in a match, Lee would in his Henley form have been a score or more lengths behind the Oxonian.

Enough can be guessed from these calculations to show that there would have been a most interesting race, to say the least, if it could have been arranged for a trial of power between Mr. Playford and Hanlan. The latter sculler used to admit, so we always understood, that the London Rowing Club sculler was the only man he had seen whom he did not feel confident of being able to beat.

To return to Hanlan's performances. The Championship of the
'World' still rested in Trickett, who had further maintained his title
(since he had beaten Sadler), by defeating Rush on the Paramatta,
Sydney, on June 30, 1877. Rush had once been the Australian
champion; Trickett had beaten him before tackling Sadler, and
this was a new attempt by Rush to regain his lost honours.
Technically, Trickett could have claimed to defend his title in his
own country; but plenty of money was forthcoming to recoup him
for expenses of travel, and he assented to meet Hanlan on the
Thames for the nominal trophy of the 'Sportsman' Challenge
Cup, but really for the wider honour of champion of the world.
The match came off on November 16, 1880, and Trickett was
defeated with even greater ease than Elliott on the Tyne.

Just about this date a sculling regatta, open to the world, was
organised on the Thames. It was got up purely for commercial
purposes by a company called the 'Hop Bitters,' who required to
advertise their wares. Nevertheless, it produced good sport.
Hanlan did not compete in it. It came off only two days after his
match with Trickett. Our British scullers took part in it and with
most humiliating results. Not one of them could gain a place in
the final heat, for which four prizes were awarded to the four
winners of trial heats. The four winners of the contest were one
and all either colonials or Americans, and the winner was one
Elias Laycock, also a Sydney man, and undoubtedly a better
sculler than Trickett, although the latter was the nominal
champion of Australia at the time. Laycock sculled in good style,
so far as leg-work and finish of the stroke; his body action was not
cramped, but he had not so long a swing as should, if possible, be
displayed by a man of his size. He scaled rather above twelve
stone. Wallace Ross, who finished second to him, after leading
him some distance, had been the favourite, and had been reputed
as only a trifle inferior to Hanlan. The forward reach and first
part of Ross's stroke was as good as could be wished, but he had a
cramped, tiring, and ugly finish with his arms and shoulders.
When Laycock succeeded in beating him a furore was created;
Laycock's staying powers were unmistakable, and many who saw
him fancied that his stamina would enable him to give Hanlan

trouble before the end of four miles. Laycock himself was not endued with so high an opinion of his own merits: but he was too game a man to shirk a contest when it was proposed to him, and the result was that he was soon matched to scull Hanlan. The match came off on the following February 14, 1881, over the Thames course. Laycock stuck to his work all the way, but was never in it for speed. Hanlan led from start to finish, and won easily.

A year later Hanlan was back in England to row Boyd on the Tyne. Boyd's friends fondly fancied that he had developed some improvement, but it was a delusion. Never was an oarsman more wedded to vicious style and wanton waste of strength than the pet of the Tyne. The race came off on April 3, 1882, and was, of course, an easy paddle for Hanlan. The knowledge that Hanlan was going to be again on English waters, brought about a return match between him and Trickett. This was rowed on the Thames on May 1 following, and once more the Canadian won easily.

No one in Britain thought fit to challenge Hanlan again, after the decisive manner in which he had disposed of all his opponents: but in his own country he twice defended his title, in 1883. On May 31 in that year he rowed J. L. Kennedy, a comparatively new man, in Massachusetts, and beat him; and on the following July 18, he once more met his old opponent, Wallace Ross, on the St. Lawrence, and beat him, though after a closer race than heretofore.

1884: NEPEAN, AUSTRALIA

*The aquatic dream of Sydney was realised, and lovers of rowing
in New South Wales had the privilege of seeing one of their best
scullers chase the champion of the world, Edward Hanlan, on
Thursday, May 22nd, over a three-mile course on the Nepean
River. A good many patrons of rowing in Sydney resented the
transfer from the usual champion course on the Parramatta River,
and the attendance was not so great as was anticipated. The race
had evidently been made the means of a big speculation, on the
chance of a great crowd visiting Penrith to see the contest. A large
space on either bank of the river was enclosed with a corrugated
iron fence, and a long grandstand, with an admission of half a
sovereign, was thrown together close to the winning post. On the
night before the race, there was very little betting on the result,
and those who had taken the long odds offered when the match
was first arranged, on the chance of Laycock becoming a stronger
favorite before the day of the race were disappointed. The short
odds had an existence only in popular gossip, and not in actual
wagers at Tattersall's. The betting was 5 to 2 against Laycock, and
before the race a well-known Melbourne bookmaker offered odds
of £400 to £100 on Hanlan, without anyone caring to accept the

---

* *Edward Hanlan, champion oarsman, with history and portrait* (Albert S. Manders &
Co., Melbourne, 1884), 23.

wager. Practically, there was no betting on the event. Hanlan's preference for the Nepean rather than the Paramatta was not difficult to comprehend on getting a fair view of the river — a beautiful stretch of water, with only a single bend, and 150 yards in width for nearly the whole journey, with not a single obstruction throughout. Hanlan's objection to the Paramatta was that an oarsman acquainted with its winding course had a decided advantage over a stranger. The Parramatta is also subject to tidal influence, and on that account local knowledge of the river was also likely to be of great value in a race. Here, however, there was an almost straightaway course, and as the weather was fine and clear the water was only disturbed by the slightest ripple. As there was only one small steamer on the river, and this was much too slow to follow the race, there was no chance of getting a complete description of the tussel but as it afterwards turned out none was required. Arrangements were made, however, for signalling with different coloured flags at various points along the course, but this was merely to indicate who was leading at this particular spot. Those who had come provided with field-glasses were fortunate, but with the naked eye it was only possible to distinguish the colors when the men were within half-a-mile of home.

Hanlan was first on the water, having at the last moment chosen his Canadian boat for the race. He was dressed in dark blue, with a red cap and stockings. As he shot out into the centre of the stream, and took a trial spin, he was warmly cheered, and as he pulled about for some time there was every opportunity of noting his style. His rowing is the perfection of mechanical grace; but if, as so frequently stated, Hanlan is able to keep the way on his boat between the strokes, there was no evidence of it on his trial pull. The champion was in the best of spirits, and chatted gaily with his friends on the bank while waiting for his opponent. In reply to inquiries, he said that he felt very well indeed, and looking at him, very few doubted it. Laycock, in Cambridge blue, then paddled out from the bank and was warmly cheered from both sides of the river. In his preliminary pull he sent his boat, "The Joker," along at a remarkable pace, and altogether sculled so neatly and vigorously that those who

had taken the odds against him were if anything reassured by the slight spurt.

Both men pulled quietly side by side down to the starting point, chatting sociably on the way. At this time the interesting point with the onlookers was whether Laycock would have the lead at any time during the race. By reason of the slight bend in the course the first mile and a half of the race was rowed out of sight and under the shadow of the high wooded hills rising from either side. This part of the contest could only be seen by those in the steamer. There were many false alarms from the crowd as different boats appeared at the far away bend four-oared skiffs even being mistaken for the light sculling shells. The starting gun was not heard and when first noticed the boats appeared coming round the bend close together, within a mile and a half of the post Hanlan was leading by about a length but the fact could only be estimated by watching the oar blades as they rose from the water. All doubt on the matter was soon settled by the hoisting of the red flag (Hanlan's colour) from a bare point near the turn, although a white handkerchief waved in the wind caused some confusion. As seen through a field glass, Hanlan appeared to sit rigidly erect in his boat, and was the more conspicuous figure as he retained his jersey while Laycock was nude to the waist. The Sydney oarsman could be seen bending backward and forward in his boat and the broad blades of his sculls as he recovered after each stroke were distinctly visible; he splashed a good deal, too, while from the Canadian craft, there was barely a ripple.

From the little steamer which carried Mr. P. J. Clark, the umpire which was judiciously started some distance ahead of the boats, the men appeared to be watching each other, and neither of them made any special exertions. As the boat neared the winning post it was only too evident that Hanlan was simply playing with his man, and it was equally clear that Laycock realised the fact. The Canadian was rowing just as easily and gracefully as he had done before starting. Robert Edwards, who had been training Hanlan, followed the race for some distance in his outrigger, but as soon as he saw the champion in front he grasped the situation and retired. The procession came along very leisurely during the last quarter of a mile, although hundreds of voices on either bank appealed to Laycock to make one more try. Whether unable or unwilling, no final spurt was, however, made, and the boats remained as they had been for the last two miles of the race. The champion dashed in his oars a little quicker for the finishing strokes, and the way in which his boat answered the effort showed that, as far as he was concerned, the race had been a very easy matter indeed. The declared result was a victory for Hanlan by a length, but this might have been increased to any number of lengths had the champion wished it.

Although the sympathies of the crowd were, of course, with the local oarsman, Hanlan was loudly cheered at the finish, his genial manner having made him a general favourite with everyone in Sydney. The applause was doubled when the Canadian, after bringing his boat dexterously alongside of his opponent, grasped him heartily by the hand. Many left the ground with the belief that Hanlan had, as usual, led from the start, but speaking to him after the race I took down a description of it, as follows:-- "Laycock led by about half a boat's length for the first quarter of a mile. Then I passed him, and kept about a length ahead for the rest of the distance." In these few words the race is fully described. The official time for the three miles 380 yards was 22m. 45s., not quite so good as has been done in some trial pulls over the same course when the men were in training.

Hanlan will leave for Melbourne tonight, for his exhibition there on Saturday, a rowing machine, in which he is able to show his style to the same effect as if in a boat, having been already sent down Those Victorians who are acquainted with the line physique of such oarsmen as Laycock, Trickett, and Rush will, on seeing Hanlan, be surprised that a man so much smaller should be able so easily to defeat the crack Australian oarsmen. The Canadian, however, has reduced rowing to a perfect science, and although he was not properly extended in this race he never, under any circumstances, seems to alter his style by quickening or decreasing the strokes as occasion may require Laycock did not maintain the form promise by his trial spin, and splashed considerably towards the close of the race. After the race, Hanlan appeared to be in no

way affected by his exertions and says that he never wishes to feel much better than he did on this occasion. After the result of yesterday's match it is not likely that any great effort will be made to arrange a second race on the Nepean, the gate money speculation having proved an utter failure. Several other races were rowed during the day and Hamerton, a young oarsman from the Clarence River, showed very good form in the skiff race, when he defeated several oarsmen of much greater repute.

THE RACE

Arrived at the Gorge both men landed, and had a few minutes rest and a rub down. Having been made cool and comfortable, Laycock was the first to step into his boat, attired principally in "buff" and blue trunks. He then went for a short preliminary to make sure that all was right and tight. Being satisfied he took up his position at the starting point, where he was shortly joined by Hanlan, dressed in his neat dark blue rowing suit and red cap. Having placed himself in a line with Laycock, not many seconds elapsed before both men dipped their sculls for the start. They got away beautifully well together, Hanlan pulling his sculls through at the rate of 30 per minute, without the slightest flurry or splash. Laycock, on the other hand, went away at the rate of 32. He seemed by no means so much at home in his boat as his opponent and knocked up a good deal of water. Laycock steadied himself and began rowing in much better form, but he was now half a length to the bad. Nearing the milepost both slowed down to 30 per minute, Hanlan leading by almost a clear length, and rowing in an easy style as if it were no exertion whatever to him. The same order was maintained to the second mile, except that Hanlan had increased his lead to two clear lengths.

The pace from the start was now telling on Laycock, who had reduced his strokes to 28, Hanlan rowing about the same. Although the latter appeared quite unconcerned and cool, the Australian was bathed in perspiration and began looking anxiously over his shoulder. By the time the third mile was reached Laycock, by a little extra pressure, managed to reduce the gap between them to a boat's length. Approaching the bridge the excitement of the spectators grew intense as Laycock was seen to be gaining on Hanlan, and a hundred yards from the winning post they were almost level. Hanlan did not allow affairs to remain in this state long. With three or four powerful strokes he shot away from Laycock and won by a bare length, amid the greatest excitement, in 22m. 45s.

PORTLAND DAILY PRESS.

ESTABLISHED JUNE 23, 1862—VOL. 23.   PORTLAND, MONDAY MORNING, OCTOBER 26, 1885.   PRICE THREE CENTS.

HANLAN HUMBLED.

Teemer Easily Defeats the Toronto Sculler.

And Is Now the Champion Oarsman of America.

Hanlan Weakens and Capsizes His Boat.

Troy, N. Y., Oct 24.[*]

The double scull race between John Teemer of McKeesport, Penn., and Edward Hanlan of Toronto, was rowed this afternoon over the Pleasure Island course, a mile and a half and return. Hanlan's defeat was glorious in the minds of a majority of the spectators, but in the opinion of his friends, he was beaten by an accident. The race was for the stakes of $2000 and the championship of America. The general impression yesterday was that Hanlan would win, or it was thought that in the strong current and high water his science would out-do Teemer's strength. All of Courtney's friends have pinned their faith to Teemer and backed him heavily. They are happy and wealthy tonight. At 3.30 o'clock, 3000 people were on Pleasant Island; as many more were on excursion boats in the river, and several

---

[*]   *Portland Daily Press,* October 26, 1885.

thousands were strung along the Hudson River railroad track on the east side.

The officers of the race were as follows; Referee, James Ormond of Boston; official time-keeper, Timothy Donoghue of Newburg; judge at the start and finish for Hanlan, Fred Plaisted; judge at the start and finish for Teemer, Wallace Ross; judge at the turn for Hanlan, Daniel Breen of Boston; Judge at the turn for Teemer, J. R. O'Regan.

Pools sold on the island showed Hanlan the favorite at $100 to $70. The betting was unusually brisk, more money changing hands than hi both of the recent double-scull races. Teemer, when weighed in his club-house, tipped the beam at 159 and Hanlan at 156. Both rowed in cedar shells made by Huddick of Boston. Teemer's boat was thirty-one feet six inches long, six inches deep and weighed twenty-nine pounds; Hanlan's boat was thirty-one feet nine inches in length, ten and one-half inches wide and weighed twenty-seven pounds. Hanlan's boat was perfectly new, never having been used before. Teemer's boat had seen some service, but had never before been used by him.

At 4.20 o'clock Hanlan launched his boat, and amid the cheers of the thousands of spectators rowed down to the starting point. Teemer quickly followed. Hanlan wore a red and white striped shirt and blue trunks. He wore no cap, while Teemer had on a dark cap, blue and white shirt and navy blue trunks.

At 4.67 the referee cautioned the oarsmen. Teemer had taken the inside position. Almost immediately afterwards the word was given. Teemer caught the water first, and started away with a rush, pulling a long, steady stroke of 34 to the minute. Hanlan in the middle of the river with the powerful current to contend with, bent to his work as he never had done in a race in this country before. He pulled thirty-eight strokes a minute, and for a mile managed to keep on even terms with Teemer. The latter seemed nervous and excited before the start, but when he got into the boat he appeared to have forgotten his fright, and rowed like a man confident of winning. The pace that Hanlan had set was telling on him more than it did on Teemer, for he began to row unsteady, and at the three-quarter mile post Teemer began to draw away from him by the foot, so that when the men passed the mile point Teemer had the lead and clear water. Teemer turned the tables on Hanlan, and he now began to spurt. "Come on," he called out, but Hanlan could not, and from this point Teemer drew away from Hanlan, and was leaving him at every stroke. Hanlan fought desperately and tried again and again to make up the lost ground, rowing 38 strokes to the (minute, but Teemer was too much for him; he had more speed and better staying powers, and as the men reached the upper stake Teemer was leading by four lengths, and had the race well in hand. Teemer was around and straightened out for home, when Hanlan, 15 seconds behind, made for his buoy. He rushed at it like a man bewildered and ran into the boat in which sat his judge at the turn, Daniel Breen. One side of the washboard of his shell cracked like a peanut shell, the boat swerved, and, pointing down stream, began to fill. Hanlan took a stroke or two and then keeled over into the water.

He was helped into a skiff. His boat was bailed out and he started for home. He was a beaten man, however, and the judge who was in Teemer's boat at the upper stake, says he was rowed out when he got there, and that he was "dead" and could not go on. Teemer reached his stakeboat at 11 m. 35 $^{1/2}$s. which is remarkable time against such a current. Hanlan reached his 11 seconds later, so that it is easily seen that Teemer had him beaten. Teemer, seeing what had happened, let up and rowed leisurely home. On his way he received quite an ovation. He paid Hanlan in his kind, stopped, threw kisses, gagged, coughed, took off his hat, and did to Hanlan what the latter has been doing to others in all his races.

Teemer said he would not make fun of any oarsman except Hanlan. Teemer, after finishing the race, rowed back to his quarters, and the people were greatly excited over him. Great crowds collected around his quarters, and he was called on for a speech. He did not want to make one, but the crowd insisted that he must say something, so he climbed up on the top of his quarters and said: "Gentlemen: I think I rowed to win this race, and shall always do so." He then jumped down, and cheer after cheer was given him.

Hanlan feels badly over his defeat, and his friends say that he cried when he got out of his boat and was greatly broken up. Hanlan backed himself, and says Teemer beat him fairly. It is usually the custom to shake hands with each other after a race. Mr. Volk, Teemer's backer, tried to have John shake hands with Hanlan, but the McKeesport lad would not do it. Teemer is happy. He has beaten Hanlan in a square, level up race, and is entitled to great credit. He leaves for home in a few days and will visit Boston in about six weeks. He, with Ross, will row any two men in the world a doublc- scull race for $2600 a side. Hanlan returned to Albany this evening. He makes no complaint, but says, "I will acknowledge that Teemer beat me." He goes to Worcester Monday and will be at the Hosmer-Laing race on Tuesday next. After that he will go home for the winter.

Teemer is now the champion, and Hanlan will have to accept his terms should they race again. Teemer rowed the course in 21m. 12s. Had he been pushed on the way home he could have beaten the record. Because Wallace Boss, Teemer's trainer is Hanlan's brother-in-law, people are saying tonight that the race was a put-up job, but Teemer's friends insist that Hanlan and Ross have been enemies for years and that the race was square. Teemer is the lion of the hour, and already plans are on foot to arrange a race between him and Beach.

LOOKS AS THOUGH IT WAS FIXED.
A SUSPICIOUS RACE BETWEEN HANLAN AND ROSS.

MONTREAL, July 1.[*] A regatta was held today on the Richelieu River, at St. Johns, about 30 miles from this city. The principal event was a race between Edward Hanlan and Wallace Ross, three miles, with a turn, for a purse of $3,000. The committee refused to allow the members of the press to follow the race in the referee's boat, and it was only by dint of considerable bullying that *The Times* correspondent was allowed to take a seat in the police boat. Even then the launch was kept a long distance behind the oarsmen, and as they were nearing the buoys it was run in close to the bank, so that the oarsmen were for the time hidden from view. In fact everything was done to prevent the race properly followed. Hanlan won the toss and chose the inside course. At the start both men went off at a terrific pace, Hanlan rowing 34 strokes and Ross 32. Hanlan at once shot ahead, and once decently away from the barge both men slacked down and sawed away leisurely, Hanlan turning the buoy a second ahead of his opponent. The next seen of them, however, Ross was several lengths ahead, and this order was maintained till within 300 yards of the finish, when Hanlan spurted and came in ahead by six or eight inches, in 21:15. The general impression was that the race had been fixed, and this was lent color to by the suspicious conduct of the committee. The time-keeper announced the time as 20:30, but even taking the outside figures, it would be next to an impossible feat if the course was the proper length, as there is a strong current to contend with, and the men were not rowing at a phenomenal rate.

---

[*] *New York Times*, July 2, 1886.

HUNTSVILLE GAZETTE.

BY HUNTSVILLE GAZETTE COMPANY.   "With Charity for All, and Malice Towards None."   SUBSCRIPTION: $1.50 per Annum

VOLUME VIII.   HUNTSVILLE, ALA., SATURDAY, JUNE 4, 1887.   NUMBER 28.

Gaudaur vs. Hanlan — Pullman, IL 1887

GAUDAUR GOT THERE. [*]

The Championship Sculling Race Between Hanlan and Gaudaur at Pullman, Ill. Results in a Victory for the St Louis[†] Man—The Race Rowed in the Rain—Hanlan Not Yet Satisfied.

CHICAGO, May 30.

The three-mile race between Edward Hanlan, the famous Canadian oarsman, and Jacob Gaudaur, of St. Louis, was contested at six o'clock this evening at Pullman, and resulted in a splendid victory for the oarsman from Missouri. The contest was for $5,000, the major portion of the gate receipts, and the championship of America. Both men were in fine form and made an interesting and exciting race. Gaudaur finished, five lengths ahead of Hanlan in 20:29, and apparently could have beaten the ex-champion by a dozen lengths had he been so disposed, but he stopped active work when in front of the grandstand and pulled to the finish line in a very slow and easy manner.

The contest attracted a great crowd of people from this city, and the town of Pullman overflowed with humanity. From ten o'clock until four stiff breezes blew over the lake, and the water ran so high that a race at all seemed impossible. At one time a furious wind storm, accompanied by rain, passed over the town, driving the spectators in-doors, and causing a universal feeling that the race would have to be postponed. But as the evening drew near the wind subsided, and the water of Lake Calumet became

---

[*] *Huntsville Gazette* (Huntsville, Ala.), vol VII, no. 28, June 4, 1887.

[†] Gaudaur wasn't from St Louis, as stated again in the article, but he was from Orillia, Ontario, and Hanlan was his mentor.

calmer, and there was a prospect of fairweather conditions for a good contest.

There were six thousand people in the grandstand, and many thousand along the shore, when shortly before six o'clock a referee Hamilton Busby, of the *Turf, Field and Farm*, of New York, appeared in the launch Jappa, and sailed for the starting bouys. A few minutes after, Gaudaur appeared in his shell, and quietly rowed to the starting place to await the arrival of Hanlan. After some delay Hanlan put in an appearance in his slender shell, wearing a blue and white striped shirt, a cap of the same material and a pair of blue knee breeches.

There was some preliminary work, and then the two oarsmen came close together and the word was given for the start. Hanlan was the first to catch the water but Gaudaur was quick to follow him, and away the two shells shot through the lake in steady motion, despite the quite heavy waves that were rolling. There was a loud outburst of applause from the vast crowd of spectators as the men swept by the grandstand and settled down to their work. Hanlan, whose course lay farthest from shore, sent his strokes up to thirty-eight to the minute, and was soon in the lead of his opponent. Gaudaur was not far behind, however, and held his own in good shape.

When the men were half a mile from the starting point, Hanlan had drawn ahead half a length, and was spurting with a short stroke. Gaudaur was pulling thirty to the minute in a steady, easy manner, not apparently worried by the champion's lead.

The wind had now freshened considerably, and a driving rain storm set in, but neither oarsman seemed to mind the rough weather, but swept along steadily and gracefully as before. Hanlan increased his lead to a length, when one mile and a quarter from the starting point; but the storm now closed around the men and nothing could be seen of them save two indistinct objects bobbing like corks in the distance. The most powerful glass could not penetrate the thick curtain of rain which was constantly falling between the oarsmen and the spectators.

Hanlan was first to turn the distance buoy, and when the rain curtain opened so that he could be seen, it was found that he still had a good lead, but was splashing to and fro in rough waves.

When about a mile from home Gaudaur, who had been lying back from one to two lengths, suddenly spurted and slowly, but surely closed the gap. Hanlan also spurted and made a determined struggle to keep the lead, but Gaudaur was still fresh after his efforts, and kept up his fast stroke, passing Hanlan harder and harder each moment. Hanlan made one more spurt and then sank back on his sculls just as he neared the grand stand, and appeared almost at a standstill.

Gaudaur shot to the front five lengths and held this plate to the finish. Gaudaur's official time was 20:29; Hanlan's, 20:31. The latter made the turn in 10:10. There was great enthusiasm shown by the friends of Gaudaur at his victory, and he was greeted with unbounded demonstrations of delight. He said it was the hardest race he had ever rowed. Hanlan said that he was beaten fairly and squarely, but that he was not yet ready to admit that Uaudaur was the better man.

*SPLENDID in her defeat, Yale's showing at Henley and Jake
Gaudaur's victory over James Stanbury in a race for international
supremacy on the Thames were the two notable aquatic events of
1896. It was expected that Yale would distinguish herself against
the pick of England's racing crews for the reason that no more
formidable aggregation of college rowing men ever sat in a boat
than the crew selected to represent America in the struggle. But a
series of unfortunate happenings, involving the illness of the men,
internal dissensions growing out of differing opinions between the
oarsmen and their coach's lack of familiarity with the changed
water conditions, etc., etc., culminated in defeat, although it must
be said to the credit of the eight men comprising the crew that
they made a game struggle against superior odds, and the
prediction was freely advanced that in another race, with equal
conditions, they would win.

The aquatic authorities at Yale were sufficiently satisfied with
the showing made by the crew to venture the belief that another
race would be arranged for 1897, providing, of course, that the
result of the intercollegiate races here justified it. Harvard will
again be a factor in the struggle, and a very determined factor.
The English stroke has been adopted, and Mr. Lehman, an

English coach, imported to teach it to the men, suggests the idea that Harvard, too, has in mind a probable trip abroad for the purpose of having a try at the Henley championship. It will all depend, however, upon the outcome of the local struggle, but the indications are that one or the other of the crews will be in the Thames struggle. There was a revival of interest in professional rowing, due mainly to Jake Gaudaur's victory over Stanbury, the Australian champion, on the Thames. Nothing has happened in the rowing world since Searle and O'Connor crossed blades for the blue ribbon on England's historical river in 1889 to cause more excitement. Professional rowing had languished lamentably during the previous six or seven years. There was a time in Australia when crackajacks kept cropping up with such rapidity that it was difficult to keep track of them; but, looking back, it seems as if the rowing spirit died in young Australia when ill-fated Harry Searle succumbed to typhoid fever shortly after his memorable race with O'Connor. Stanbury, who was an acknowledged rival of Searle in the latter's best days, soon established his right to wear the champion's shoes, and for many years he has been left in undisputed possession of them. There was a flicker of interest when Tom Sullivan, the New Zealander, blossomed out as a championship candidate, but Sullivan proved only a flash in the pan. He was defeated in England, and the talk of a match between him and Stanbury ceased suddenly, the champion being compelled to rest on his oars and wait vainly for challengers. For a number of years the only interest that rowing held for Englishmen grew out of the fact that the big races were rowed on the Thames.

The old country could not turn out material fit to cope with the Beaches, the Hanlans, the Searles and O'Connors that Australia and Canada produced, and all that London could do on red-letter rowing days was to furnish the river and the spectators. But when little Wag Harding came to town—he weighed but 140 pounds and was regarded as the best bit of British stuff seen in half a score of years—the Londoners held their heads aloft and congratulated one another on the prospect of England regaining her old-time rowing supremacy.

They backed "Wag" against big, lumbering, easy-going Stanbury, and the Australian simply rowed rings around his diminutive rival. Gaudaur then tried to induce the antipodean sculler to come to America for a race, but he refused, and the only alternative left to the Orillia champion, who had just beaten Hanlan, Bubear and Barry at Halifax, was to go to England. The race was simply no race at all after the preliminary spurt. Gaudaur won handily, upsetting the calculations of the Solons of the aquatic world, who predicted a hollow victory for Stanbury.

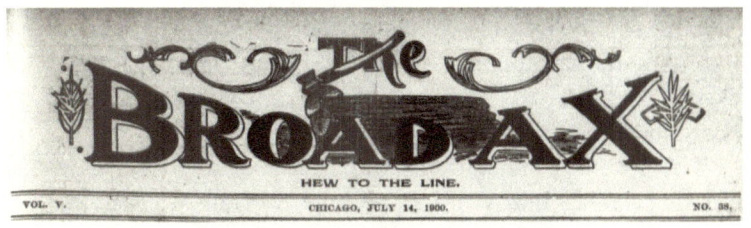

HEW TO THE LINE.

VOL. V.   CHICAGO, JULY 14, 1900.   NO. 38.

ROWED IN 200 RACES.
NED HANLAN AGAIN LOOKING FOR THE CHAMPIONSHIP.

He Has Just Issued a Challenge to His Former Antagonist, Jake Gaudaur to Scull for World's Leadership—Story of His Victories. *

No oarsman on this side of the water ever became so well known as Edward Hanlan, former champion sculler of the world, and one of the best men who ever sat in a shell. Interest is now revived in the ex-champion from the fact that he has issued a challenge to his old antagonist, Jake Gaudaur, for a race in Boston. Although many years at the game Hanlan is still able to do a fast sprint. Ned Hanlan is now 44 years of age.

He was born in Toronto, Ont, and learned to row almost as early as he did to walk. His racing career dates from 1872, when he won two single scull races. Hanlan rowed his first race out of his own country in 1876 at Philadelphia and won three heats in as many days. He also cut down the record for the three-mile course to 21m. 9s. In 1878, he won the championship of America by defeating Evan Morris over the Hulton course at Pittsburg. He also defeated Charles Courtney the same year. The next year Hanlan

EDWARD HANLAN. (As the once famous oarsman appears today.)

journeyed to England and Africa.

*   *The Broad Ax* (Salt Lake City, Utah; Chicago, Ill.), July 14, 1900, p.2.

He surprised the people on the other side by defeating their crack professionals, Hawdon and Elliott. In England, in 1879, he gave his first exhibition as a sculler. Over a five-mile course he cut the record from 35m. 10s. to 33m. $5^{1/4}$s.

The next year Hanlan won the championship of the world and the cup. The next year he won from Laycock of Australia, previously defeated by him, and became the owner of the famous *Sportsman's Cup*. In July, 1883, he broke the world's record for four miles, making it in 27m. 57s. In 1884, Hanlan met his first defeat at the hands of Beach, losing the championship of the world through the interference of the steamer Tonki. He was defeated for the second time by Beach the same year. Hanlan went after the three-mile record the next year and succeeded in lowering it from 19m. 54s. to 19m. 23s. In 1887, Hanlan lost the championship of America to Gaudaur at Lake Calumet, Pullman, Ill. A return match was later made with Gaudaur and again Hanlan won the championship of America.

Going to Australia once more. Beach again won from him and turned the title over to Kemp, who was successful in defending it. Since 1893, Hanlan has done little rowing, barely enough to keep himself in condition. Most of his time being devoted to coaching. He is now coach for the Union Boat Club of Boston.

During his career as a sculler Hanlan has rowed in 200 races, and of these, only four were lost by him through out-and-out rowing. In nearly every case in which he failed to finish first it was through some accident. In Australia, he was defeated by Beach, but the latter was so rowed out at the finish that he was carried from his boat and this in his own climate and on the river in which he had been accustomed to row. Nearly 100 of Hanlan's races have been for the championship. In these matches alone his earnings were over $80,000, and these and other races and exhibitions netted him at least $350,000.

NOTE: It doesn't appear that this race ever materialized, but the fact that such a race — a duel between two Canadians — was advertised in a Utah newspaper, which was to take place in Boston, says something about the efforts to draw the whole continent into rowing, likely for the sake of raising stakes.

APPENDIX

*Anno Regni Victoriæ, Britanniarum Reginæ,
Decimo Sexto & Decimo Septimo.*

An Act for the Suppression of Betting Houses.

[20th August 1853]*

(16 & 17 Vict.) CAP. CXIX.

WHEREAS a kind of Gaming has of late sprung up tending
to the Injury and Demoralization of improvident Persons by the
opening of Places called Betting Houses or Offices, and the
receiving of Money in advance by the Owners or Occupiers of
such Houses or Offices, or by other Persons acting on their Behalf,
on their Promises to pay Money on Events of Horse Races and
the like Contingencies:' For the Suppression thereof, be it enacted
by the Queen's most Excellent Majesty, by and with the Advice
and Consent of the Lords Spiritual and Temporal, and
Commons, in this present Parliament assembled, and by the
Authority of the same, as follows:

*No House, &c. to be kept for Purpose of Owner or Occupier betting with
other Persons.*

No House, Office, Room, or other Place shall be opened, kept,
or used for the Purpose of the Owner, Occupier, or Keeper
thereof, or any Person using the same, or any Person procured or
employed by or acting for or on behalf of such Owner, Occupier,
or Keeper, or Person using the same, or of any Person having the
Care or Management or in any Manner conducting the Business
thereof betting with Persons resorting thereto; or for the Purpose
of any Money or valuable Thing being received by or on behalf
of such Owner, Occupier, Keeper, or Person as aforesaid as or for
the Consideration for any Assurance, Undertaking, Promise, or
Agreement, express or implied, to pay or give thereafter any
Money or valuable Thing on any Event or Contingency of or

---

*   https://vlex.co.uk/vid/betting-act-1853-861251439

relating to any Horse Race, or other Race, Fight, Game, Sport, or Exercise, or as or for the Consideration for securing the paying or giving by some other Person of any Money or valuable Thing on any such Event or Contingency as aforesaid; and every House, Office, Room, or other Place opened, kept, or used for the Purposes aforesaid, or any of them, is hereby declared to be a common Nuisance and contrary to Law.

THE BETTING ACT—ARRESTS AT NEWCASTLE.

HC Deb: 29 May 1883 vol 279 cc1100-1*

MR. JOHN MORLEY asked the Secretary of State for the Home Department, Whether his attention has been drawn to the action of the police in Newcastle on Tyne on the 23rd instant, in entering two public houses and there arresting sixty-nine persons, of whom sixty-four were shortly afterwards unconditionally released; and, whether he will take steps to discourage too stringent an application of the Betting Act?§

SIR WILFRID LAWSON wished to ask this further Question —Whether the right hon. Gentleman would take steps to put down betting among the gentlemen who frequented Tattersall's?§

SIR WILLIAM HARCOURT, in reply, said, with the leave of the House he would answer the Question on the Paper. His hon. Friend (Mr. J. Morley) must know that he (Sir William Harcourt) had no control of the Newcastle-on-Tyne police, nor could he prescribe to the magistrates of Newcastle how they should perform their duty in the administration of the law. If he were to offer advice in a case where he had no power, it would be of no avail. With regard to the latter part of the Question, his hon. Friend was, no doubt, acquainted with the local authorities, and,

---

having great influence, could enforce on them the views he entertained on the subject.§

Subsequently,

MR. JOSEPH COWEN wished to ask a Question of the Home Secretary with reference to his answer to his Colleague concerning the police raids on betting men at Newcastle. As he understood, the right hon. and learned Gentleman refused to interfere with this matter on the ground that he had no control over the police at Newcastle. Identical proceedings took place within half-a-mile of the Home Office every day, and he had control over the Metropolitan Police. He wished to know whether the right hon. and learned Gentleman's answer amounted to approval of the action of the Newcastle magistrates; and, if so, whether he meant to apply the same law to the betting establishments near the Home Office?§

SIR WILLIAM HARCOURT said, that he could answer for the action of the police over whom he had control; but he was unable to answer, either by way of approval or disapproval, for police over whom he had no control. If he were to express a judgment in this case upon the action of the Municipal authorities of Newcastle, he must consider the matter in an official way. He had not at present official information before him; and he could, therefore, express neither approbation nor condemnation of conduct he had not had an opportunity of considering.§

SIR WILFRID LAWSON observed, that the Question put by the hon. Member for Newcastle had not been answered. The Question was, whether the Home Secretary would take the same action with reference to the betting establishments in London, which were under his control, as had been taken with regard to those of Newcastle, over which he had no control?

DEFINING 'AMATEUR'

Definition of an Amateur. [*]

An amateur oarsman or sculler must be an officer of Her Majesty's army or navy or civil service, a member of the liberal professions, or of the Universities or Public schools, or of any established Boat- or Rowing-Club not containing mechanics or professionals; and must not have competed in any competition for either a stake, or money, or entrance-fee, or with or against a professional for any prize; nor have ever taught, pursued, or assisted in the pursuit of athletic exercises of any kind as a means of livelihood; nor have ever been employed in or about boats or in manual labour; nor be a mechanic, artisan, or labourer.

Henley Definition, April 8, 1879.

No person shall be considered an amateur oarsman or sculler: First, who has ever competed in any open competition for a stake, money, or entrance fee; secondly, who has ever competed with or against a professional for any prize; thirdly, who has ever taught, pursued, or assisted in athletic exercises of any kind as a means of gaining a livelihood; fourthly, who has been employed in or about

---

[*]   The following English, French, and German definitions and Dutch commentary are found in, Pieter Helbert Damsté and Frans Eduard Pels Rijcken, *Nederlandsch handboek voor roeisport* [Dutch manual for rowing sports] (Amsterdam: H.G. Bom, 1886), 11-14.

boats for money or wages; fifthly, is or has been by trade or employment, for wages, a mechanic, artisan or labourer.

Classification des rameurs.

Ne seront admis dans les courses d'amateurs, que les rameurs amateurs faisant partie des Sociétés invitées.

Ne sont pas amateurs:

1. Les watermen, c'est-à-dire les rameurs, faisant profession de courir.

2. Les rameurs courant ou ayant couru à gages.

3. Les marins, mariniers, passeurs, pêcheurs par état, gardiens de garages, ouvrier constructeurs de bateaux, enfin toutes les personnes, tirant leur moyen d'existence d'une façon habituelle et continuelle dans les chantiers de construction et sur les bateaux.

[translation]

Classification of Rowers.

Only amateur rowers who are part of the invited Societies will be admitted to amateur races. Non-amateurs:

1. Watermen, that is to say rowers, who make a profession of racing.

2. Rowers who have or are currently transporting for wages.

3. Sailors, boatmen, ferrymen, commercial fishermen, garage keepers, boat builders, in short, all people earning their livelihood in a habitual and continuous way at construction sites and on boats.

Deutscher Amateur-Begriff.

Amateur ist Jeder, der das Rudern nur aus Liebhaberei mit eigenen Mitteln betreibt oder betrieben hat und dafür keinerlei Vermögensvortheile in Aussicht hat oder hatte, weder als Arbeiter seinen Lebensunterhalt lediglich durch seiner Hände-Arbeit verdient, noch in irgend einer Weise beim Bootbau beschäftigt ist. Wer um Geldpreise startet oder nach dem 1 Januar 1884 gestartet hat, wird nicht als Amateur betrachtet.

German Amateur Definition. [translation]

An amateur is anyone who rows purely as a hobby with their own resources or and has no prospect of any financial benefits from this, neither does he earn his living as a worker solely with his hands, nor is he employed in boat building in any way. Anyone who competes for cash prizes or who competed after January 1, 1884 will not be considered an amateur.

[translation from Dutch]

We already know something about *professionals* and would like to learn about remarkable events that happened among them in England, America and Australia. In other countries, where rowing is not yet practiced by the lower classes [*volksklasse*], professional rowing does not occur. Yet the most famous professionals are largely people from the working class and, when they have achieved a certain degree of skill, are usually enabled by wealthy admirers to devote themselves entirely to it, so that one reads that when two people competing for a thousand pounds sterling, one should not think that they themselves have wagered this sum; those funds are then passed on to the *backers* from each party. Just as here a sportsman runs his horses in a race, so clubs composed of wealthy Americans have their rowers.

There are of course exceptions to this: there are also amateurs, who have made it so far as to become professionals because they have measured up against other professional rowers.

In England, certain competitions are also held annually for this class of rowers, such as the one that has existed since 1854. *Thames National Regatta* and the one founded in 1868, the *Thames Regatta*. Then there are wealthy enthusiasts, especially in America, who organize such competitions: even the *Hop Bitters Company* has already donated 5,000 dollars for that purpose several times! A truly American way of advertising, against which the *maandbladen tegen de kwakzalverij* [periodicals against quackery] will find it difficult to compete…

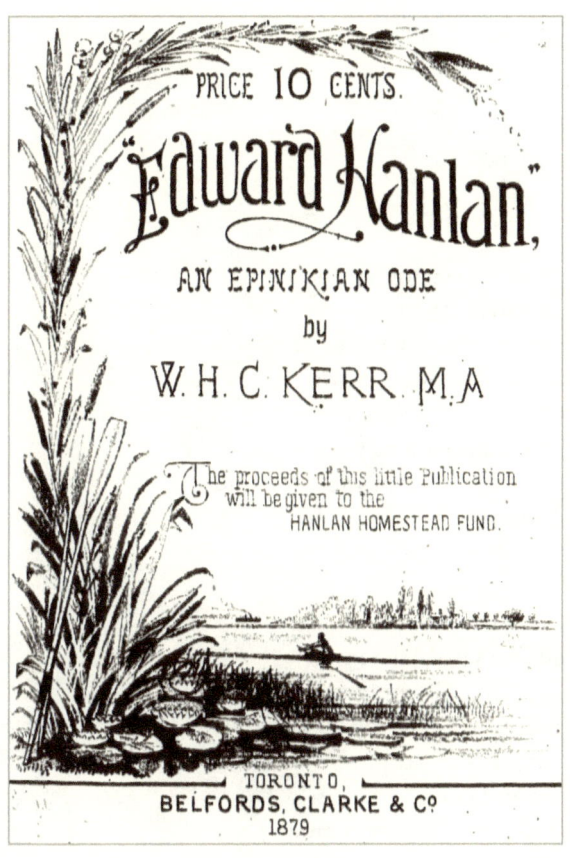

PRICE 10 CENTS.

"Edward Hanlan,"

AN EPINIKIAN ODE

by

W. H. C. KERR. M.A

The proceeds of this little Publication
will be given to the
HANLAN HOMESTEAD FUND.

TORONTO,
BELFORDS, CLARKE & Cº
1879

an epic poem (1879)*

I. HAIL to the champion sculler!
    Toronto's manly son,
    Who, across the line, and on the Tyne,
    Hath famous victories won!
    And with three cheers for Hanlan,
    The champion of the oar,
    Let us shout, Hurrah for Canada

---

* W.H.C. Kerr, *Hanlan's Record: an epic poem* (Toronto: Belfords, Clarke & Co., 1879).

The land which such hero bore.

II. In ancient Greece the victor,
    Who at Olympia strove,
    Was crowned with wreaths of olive
    In Jove's all-hallowed grove:
    His person was held sacred,
    Kings his companions were
    And envied the fate of the happy state
    Which claimed him for its heir.

III. At Pytho and at Corinth,
    The athlete's prize who won,
    Shed glory on his country,
    His kindred, and his town;
    His statue in the temples,
    In ivory and gold,
    By the side of gods and heroes
    The gymnast's prowess told.

IV. Returning to his people
    Fresh bays the conqueror waits
    The city battered down its walls
    To make him wider gates,
    And joyous crowds in triumph
    The champion bore along,
    While a Pindar sang his praises,
    In loftiest strains of song.

V. But no victor at Olympia,
    Nor by the Isthmian strand,
    Ever received such welcome
    On reaching his own land,
    As that awaits the champion
    Who ploughs the Atlantic's foam,
    With impatient keel and heart right leal
    Returning to his home.

VI. Save that no worthy poet
    For him shall wreathe a lay,
    Since none with equal laurels
    Such victor garland may.
    He won at the Centennial, And by Ohio's waves,
    And where the Eastern river
    Past Hampton seaward raves.

VII. Toronto, Pittsburg, Barrie,
    The City, "Quaker" hight.
    And the lovely Bay of Burlington
    Bear witness of his might.
    He won in every contest At each regatta won,
    Till at Lachine he overcame,
    Columbia's foremost son.

VIII. Now, shame on the foul slander
    Of those who meanly tried,
    At Courtney's cost to pander
    To a boastful people's pride;
    For Courtney was defeated,
    Not for the want of will,
    Nor by the bribe of treason,
    But by superior skill.

IX. From sea to sea victorious,
    He left his home a while,
    To gather bays more glorious
    In Britain's sea-girt isle ;
    And how he played with Hawdon,
    And how sponged out his shell,
    With tears of mirth and laughter,
    The Tyneside pitmen tell.

X. Last, matched with England's champion,
    On Tyne's excited tide,
    To see his daily practice
    They flocked from far and wide
    Each touting wharfside ranger
    The mystic magic sought,
    Which the Canadian stranger
    Had lurking in his boat.

XI. With air-bags and machinery,
    The miners stoutly held,
    Or by some secret influence,
    His skiff must be propelled
    For never such a sculler.
    Of form so lithe and fine,
    Or such modest mien, had yet been seen
    On the Thames, or on the Tyne.

XII.But no man knows save Hanlan,
    If even Hanlan knows,
    How fast his bark can travel
    When at his best he rows
    Like the flight of an eagle's pinions,
    When to the sun he soars,
    Is the graceful sweep and powerful stroke
    Of his well-feather'd oars.

XIII. Now, not a few such striplings
    This broad Dominion rears;
    Since Wallace Ross and Warren Smith
    Are well nigh Hanlan's peers.
    Girded with North-star vigour,
    And nurtured by the sea.
    By mountain, lake and river,
    A hardy brood they be.

XIV. West of the Rocky Mountains,
　　Such youth you may behold
　　Braving the Fraser's rapids,
　　In venturous quest of gold
　　And where Muskoka's camp-fires
　　Cast up a ruddy glare;
　　Where Madawaska's springtide floods
　　Their floating forests bear;

XV. Where Montmorenci's bridal veil
　　Its shower of pearls displays;
　　And where thro' mountain-gorges green
　　The Metapedia strays.
　　These eastward turned and waited
　　Impatient for the day,
　　When their compatriot might win
　　Tyne's championship away.

XVI. The day has come! From midnight
　　Until the dawn broke clear,
　　Crowds lined the banks in serried ranks
　　And every wharf and pier
　　With craft of all descriptions
　　The river was alive
　　Each bridge with human beings
　　Swarmed like a great bee-hive.

XVII. The champions take their stations,
    Promptly each takes his place,
    In the sight of all the nations
    Of the Anglo-Saxon race.
    "Now, three to one," roared Elliott,
    "That I lead all the way!"
    And his stalwart arm and lusty form
    Might feebler foe dismay.

XVIII. Such challenge disregarded
    Might not unnerve the youth,
    Whose speech on the unwon victory
    Was written out, good sooth!
    The boast was scarcely uttered,
    "They're off!" the umpire cried,
    And away they sped, but Hanlan led
    With oars superbly plied.

XIX. Like arrow from the bowstring,
    Swiftly he sped along
    Past Grindstone Quay, past Redheugh Bridge
    And all the astonished throng,
    Past the meadow-isle, whose human tides,
    Like billows, sway and roll,
    And by ten good lengths a winner.
    Swept gaily past the goal.

XX. Then from the river's crowded banks,
    From roof-top, bridge, and pier,
    Thrice thirty thousand lusty throats
    Sent up a mighty cheer;
    And many a British city
    Caught up the wild acclaim,
    And the Western world from sea to sea
    Resounded with his fame.

XXI. And while St. Lawrence to the Gulf
    Majestic takes his way;
    While through the Thousand Islands
    His sunlit waters play
    While soft auroras chase the stars
    Athwart our Northern skies
    While Indian summer tints the woods
    With iridescent dyes

XXII. While the maidens shall weave chaplets
    In Huron's maple dells;
    While o'er Rimouski's jewelled snows
    Shall ring the Christmas bells;
    While great Niagara's thunder-stroke
    Th' affrighted rocks shall shake
    While the long moonbeams nightly play
    Across Ontario's lake;

XXIII. While Ottawa, from storied cliff,
    Uplifts her crown of towers
    While modest merit still shall charm
    This Canada of ours;
    So long in distant story.
    As time rolls on apace,
    Shall it be told by young and old
    How Hanlan won the race.

XXIV.
    Now three good cheers for Hanlan!
    Our flag to the breeze unfurl'd,
    For the Champion of two continents,
    The champion of the world!
    And three times three for Canada,
    Land of the brave and free,
    The youngest of the nations:
    The Home of Liberty.

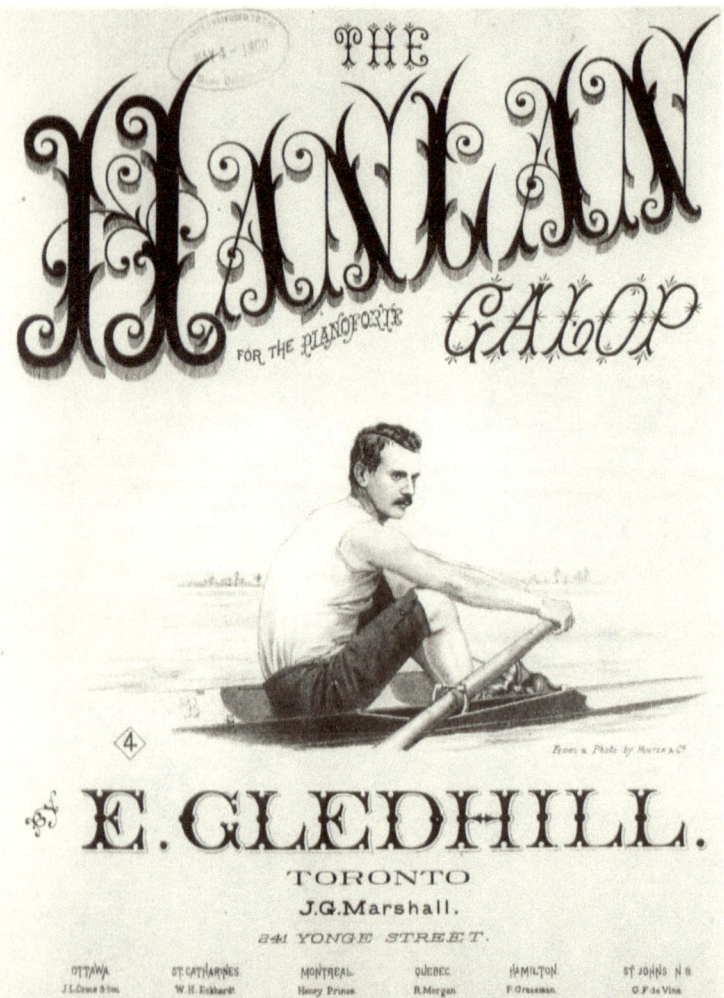

E. Gledhill, The Hanlan Galop. *Toronto: Marshall, J. G, 1878.*

THE

Hanlan Galop.

By E. GLEDHILL.

INCONCLUSIVE UNSCIENTIFIC POSTSCRIPT

ON WORKING SMARTER, NOT HARDER

JONATHAN SEILING

HARDER OR SMARTER?

Ned Hanlan is arguably the examplar of the now-overused saying, "work smarter, not harder." To be sure, he worked hard, but he probably played even harder. And while some of his playfulness was considered more "smart-ass" than smarty-pants, there's no doubt his attention to technique and innovation helped him win the day and impact the way the sport evolved.

But who actually invented the phrase? Some attribute it to Allen F. Morgenstern, an industrial engineer and the creator of the "work simplification program" in the 1930s. Can we find evidence that Morgenstern was a devotee of Hanlan's rowing prowess? Probably not.

If asked, Hanlan might retort, why does the phrase use the word "not", as if one must choose one or the other? Is there actually a preferable option of smart-yet-lazy or stupid-yet-arduous? Obviously not!

Until the day when a papyrus with the Latin words *prudentius non durius** (see attempt at a rough Gaelic rendition below), surfaces from Celtic archives, we might assume this ingenious idea was originally expressed by Ned's forebears.

**obair níos cliste ní níos deacra*